ITINERANT TEACHING

Tricks of the Trade for Teachers of Blind and Visually Impaired Students

Jean E. Olmstead

American Foundation for the Blind • New York

Itinerant Teaching: Tricks of the Trade for Teachers of Blind and Visually Impaired Students

is ©1991 by
American Foundation for the Blind
15 West 16th Street
New York, NY 10011

The American Foundation for the Blind (AFB) is a national nonprofit organization that advocates, develops, and provides programs and services to help blind and visually impaired people achieve independence with dignity in all sectors of society.

Printed in the United States of America

95 94 93   5 4 3 2

Library of Congress Cataloging-in-Publication Data
Olmstead, Jean E., 1943–
    Itinerant teaching: tricks of the trade for teachers of blind and visually
impaired students/Jean Olmstead; [photographs by Natalie Knott].
      p. cm.
    Includes index.
    ISBN 0-89128-190-8
    1. Visually handicapped children—Education—United States.
    2. Teachers of the blind—Training of—United States.   3. Visiting
teachers—Training of—United States.   I. Title.
HV1631.046 1991   91-8392
                                                    CIP

Cover art by Elizabeth Jennewine Watson

Photographs by Natalie Knott

Dedication

THIS BOOK is dedicated to itinerant teachers,

Who spend a lot of time behind the windshields of their cars,

Who carry bulky, delicate materials in and out of schools, often in inclement weather,

Who can turn the dingiest hole in the wall into a cheery classroom,

Who have the special opportunity to work with students on a one-to-one basis for periods of two to three years at a time,

Who can switch from working with a preschooler to working with a gifted high school senior and provide meaningful lessons to both,

Who answer patiently every time someone in the faculty room assumes they are substitute teachers and asks, "Who are you today?"

Who are organized, dedicated, and self-motivated,

Who are safe drivers and good map readers,

Who recognize that having a sense of humor is a survival skill,

Who realize that they have assumed their roles because they are helpers and that they are most successful when their students help themselves,

Who are patient but know when to be impatient, and

Who rise to the challenge of being itinerant because they believe that neighborhood schools are the appropriate placement for their visually impaired students.

Contents

Foreword by William F. Gallagher — vii

Acknowledgments — viii

Introduction — 1

Chapter 1. The History and Philosophy of Itinerant Teaching — 3

Chapter 2. The Itinerant Teacher: Being Effective — 5

Chapter 3. A Typical Year — 9

Chapter 4. Facilitating Integration — 39

Chapter 5. Organization of Information and Materials — 47

Chapter 6. Organization of the Program — 53

Chapter 7. Relationships and Responsibilities in Schools — 67

Chapter 8. Your Rights in Schools — 69

Chapter 9. Other Essentials — 73

Chapter 10. A Rural Perspective by Jane Stewart — 81

Appendix A. Sources of Materials and Equipment — 87

Appendix B. Organizations Serving Visually Impaired People — 91

Appendix C. Classification System for Materials — 96

Appendix D. Reference Library — 100

Appendix E. Sample Forms — 104

Index — 123

About the Authors — 127

Foreword

WHEN MOST PEOPLE hear the word "mainstreaming," they think of an abstract concept having to do with federal legislation. Some may think of the children involved. But hardly anyone thinks of the individuals who have made it possible for blind and visually impaired children to have neighborhood schools as a part of their world—itinerant teachers.

Itinerant teachers, who travel from school to school, negotiate the complicated and often frustrating ins and outs of the educational system, provide individualized instruction to students, and consult with school personnel and parents, are the unsung heroes and heroines of mainstreaming. Years ago, before the impetus for mainstreaming was a force in our society, most children with impaired vision spent a good part of their lives in residential schools. But we have come a long way from those times, and today blind and visually impaired children have a variety of educational options in addition to residential schools: nearly 90 percent of these students live at home and attend local schools along with their sighted friends. We have itinerant teachers to thank for this progress.

Many of us believe that neighborhood schools are usually the appropriate placement for blind and visually impaired students—or at least that this placement should be available as an option for students who would benefit from and are able to attend neighborhood schools. But providing support, adapted materials, one-on-one instruction, and other assistance to students with visual impairments who are attending local schools—and often traveling long distances among the different schools—is a complicated job. Therefore, we at the American Foundation for the Blind (AFB) are happy to provide support in turn to itinerant teachers. *Itinerant Teaching: Tricks of the Trade for Teachers of Blind and Visually Impaired Students* is full of suggestions and information to help make itinerant teachers more effective and their lives a bit easier. We hope that new and experienced teachers alike find in it the insider know-how and useful tips that will help them continue to make a difference in the lives of children who are blind or visually impaired.

William F. Gallagher
President and Executive Director
American Foundation for the Blind

Acknowledgments

MANY ITINERANT TEACHERS and other individuals have not only contributed to the ideas in this book but have also given me support, feedback, and affirmation during its development. I acknowledge their expert advice and willingness to help.

Many of the ideas and strategies suggested in this book evolved as a result of a group effort by itinerant members of the Visually Impaired Program in the Richmond Unified School District in Richmond, California, to provide services to visually impaired students as effectively and efficiently as possible. I extend my special appreciation to the most recent itinerant teachers—Janet Dunlop, Cinda Hubbard, Natalie Knott, Sue Loy, and Karen Yamamoto—for their dedication and creativity and to the secretary-transcriber, Ann Kelt, for her efforts in keeping the program running smoothly. I also thank my friends and my daughter, Adrienne, for their encouragement, understanding, and support.

Jane Stewart, an itinerant teacher/coordinator in Illinois, contributed valuable suggestions from a rural perspective that appear as the last chapter in this book and allowed the use of the cover sketch, a gift to her from a friend, Elizabeth Jennewine Watson. The photographs in the book were taken by Natalie Knott of Martinez, California.

—J.E.O.

Introduction

ALTHOUGH we itinerant teachers receive a lot of information about visual conditions, assessment, curriculum, and adaptations for visually impaired students, we often have to develop our own strategies and techniques to be effective and efficient while serving students at several sites because few structural guidelines exist for us. The goal of this book is not to reiterate information available in college courses and publications; rather, it is to give you nitty-gritty, practical suggestions you can use as an itinerant teacher.

In the following pages I use the term "visually impaired" to cover the entire range of visual functioning from mild visual impairment to total blindness. I have suggested strategies for working with visually impaired students that are effective in the area where I teach. Different practices may be prevalent where you work. Utilize the ideas that are in accordance with the customs in your area. Likewise, I have included sample letters and forms in several sections to demonstrate how they can make our jobs easier. The forms appear filled in, as we have used them (all the names of people and places are fictitious; resemblance to actual persons and schools is unintentional and coincidental). Adapt and use those that will be helpful to you; enlarge those you wish for readers who use large print. Blank forms are in Appendix E if you wish to use them as they are.

I hope that new itinerant teachers find my suggestions to be pertinent and valuable but not overwhelming. Take your time to settle into the job, and utilize the strategies that seem to fit your situation as you develop your style and techniques. For those who are more experienced, I hope you find some helpful hints and—more important—validation for the good job you have been doing.

Chapter 1

The History and Philosophy of Itinerant Teaching

EDUCATION of visually impaired students in the United States has changed greatly since the first residential schools for blind children were opened in the 1830s. Early in the twentieth century, local school districts established special classes for visually impaired pupils, enabling some children to live at home. Next, local districts instituted resource room programs; some of the students were enrolled in regular classes and went to the resource room for special assistance. A natural outgrowth of community-based educational programs were the itinerant programs begun in California in 1938 and in New Jersey in 1943.

Regular education students who receive itinerant services live at home and attend their neighborhood schools, where their educational needs are met by regular classroom teachers in cooperation with a traveling (itinerant) teacher who is certified to teach visually impaired students. (Visually impaired students who are enrolled in other special education classes receive similar support from a teacher of visually impaired students.) The itinerant teacher travels from school to school, providing special materials, consultation with school personnel, and individualized instruction.

Placement in the itinerant program is appropriate for students who can benefit from extensive participation in regular class activities, will use adapted materials and special equipment and techniques, and can function as members of a regular class when conditions may be less than ideal for fulfilling their special needs. Because not every ditto will be adapted for them and not every peer will be understanding and accepting, the visually impaired students must be able to adjust to a variety of conditions and reactions.

Despite the occasional limitations of placement in regular classes, visually impaired students who are served by itinerant teachers may benefit from the extra support inherent in attending schools with their siblings and long-standing neighborhood friends. Because they live at home and are not usually subjected to long daily bus rides, they may participate more readily in after-school and community programs and enjoy more solid relationships with their families. Their parents may find it easier to participate in school activities because the school is nearby and familiar to them. In short, these visually impaired students interact in the kind of environment in which they will later live and work.

Itinerant programs, resource rooms, special classes, and residential schools all have their places in the continuum of services for visually impaired students. Each option has its

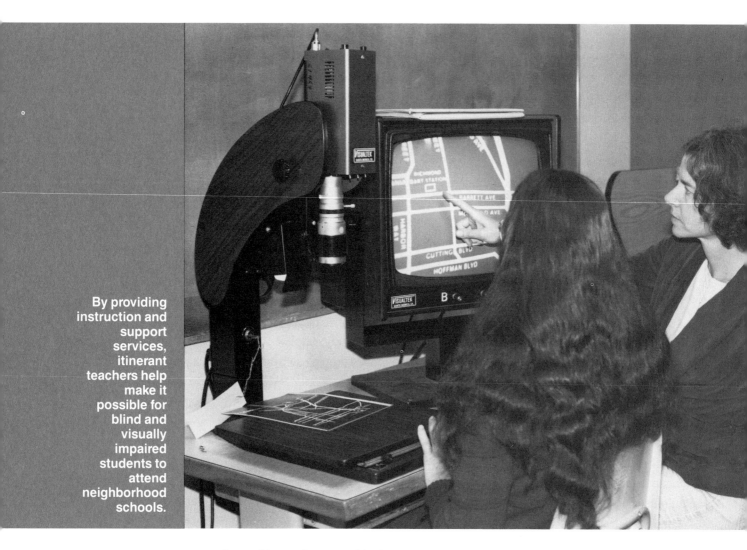

By providing instruction and support services, itinerant teachers help make it possible for blind and visually impaired students to attend neighborhood schools.

strengths and its weaknesses. Each option should be available to every student according to his or her needs and abilities, as determined by the Individualized Education Program (IEP) developed for the student in accordance with the Education for All Handicapped Children Act. Careful, ongoing, systematic assessment provides information that allows the team working on a student's IEP to make a judicious decision about which program will be the most appropriate placement for this particular student.

Ideally, no child should be locked into one particular program but should have the option of alternative placement as his or her needs change. Some students in resource rooms, special classes, or residential schools may move to itinerant programs as they acquire the skills necessary for greater independence. Some students in itinerant programs may benefit from spending a year or two or even a summer in one of the other settings to receive the more concentrated instruction and support that are difficult to provide on an itinerant basis. This flow among different programs is essential to providing services that will fulfill the potential of each student.

Chapter 2

The Itinerant Teacher: Being Effective

WHEN NEW CLASSROOM TEACHERS arrive at their first assignment, they are usually assigned a room and a mailbox, a group of students who are relatively homogeneous at least according to age, a set of textbooks and teachers' manuals, classroom equipment and supplies, and a bell schedule. I do not imply that the first year or so of teaching is easy, but new classroom teachers have a fair amount of structure to help them develop their competence.

In comparison, new itinerant teachers usually have to establish their own structure. Sometimes the only information they receive is a list of students, who may range in ability from severely handicapped to gifted, vary in age from birth to 21, and be located at several sites that may or may not be in close geographic proximity. New itinerant teachers gather information from school records and observations. They consult with classroom teachers and school administrators to set up a schedule in which the best times to pull students out of their classes are coordinated with the times that appropriate rooms are available for their use, move materials and equipment into each school, and determine which needs of the students they will address.

To be effective, itinerant teachers

■ Utilize or develop school or community resources to help with important areas, such as living skills, recreational and leisure activities, and motor development, that may be difficult to address because of the limited time they can spend at each site,

■ Serve as liaisons among the students, parents, school personnel, and medical, community, and professional resources,

■ Establish rapport and take a cooperative, flexible, yet assertive approach because the relationships they foster are vital to the successful mainstreaming of their students,

■ Are observant and use their ingenuity, creativity, and intuition to facilitate their students' integration,

■ Have a keen understanding of people and are able to communicate with people of a wide range of ages, abilities, and backgrounds,

Key Skills and Tasks

- Keep abreast of resources, new technology, and trends in the educational field by attending conferences and receiving information from organizations and businesses that serve visually impaired people,

- Perform functional vision assessments for referrals to the program for visually impaired students,

- Maintain a realistic perspective about what they can accomplish,

- Do their best to anticipate problems before they arise, and

- Work well both on an individual basis and as members of a team.

In addition, for visually impaired students to be effectively served in an itinerant program, at least three basic factors should be true. Therefore, I have assumed the following in presenting the material in this book:

1. *The visually impaired students enrolled in regular education classes and served in the itinerant program are appropriately placed.* To meet the needs of individual students, a range of placement options should be available: an itinerant program, a resource room, a special class for visually impaired students, and a residential school. The IEP team, with input from all its members, decides which placement is appropriate for a student at a particular time. The student may move from one placement to another as his or her needs and abilities change.

   For visually impaired students enrolled in regular education classes, itinerant placement is indicated when a student can function independently at an appropriate academic level, utilize special equipment and adaptive techniques, and display adequate skills in activities of daily living and socialization when the itinerant teacher is not at the site. Therefore, if a student is exhibiting age-appropriate behavior and measurable, continuous academic progress, itinerant placement is suitable even though the student may require relatively extensive intervention from the itinerant teacher.

2. *The itinerant teachers in a program have realistic, manageable caseloads.* Administrators and teachers alike need to recognize that caseloads can fluctuate widely. The number of students an itinerant teacher can serve effectively depends on the students' needs and the travel time generated by the caseload, as well as on the number of referrals to the program for visually impaired students. When the students need less intervention and are closely grouped geographically, the teacher may be able to mainstream 14 students successfully. However, if the students need extensive support (including more direct instruction, many adapted materials, and more consultation and observation), 5 students may be all that the teacher can serve adequately.

   The support system in the program can also affect the itinerant teachers' caseload. The presence of orientation and mobility (O&M) instructors, transcribers, and aides and up-to-date equipment may allow the teachers to serve more students.

   Working conditions are seldom delineated for itinerant personnel in teachers' union contracts with school districts. Generally, all classroom teachers have a clearly defined teaching day that includes a conference-preparation period and a lunch break.

An array of equipment sent to a site for a student, the itinerant teacher, and an aide-transcriber. Planning and coordination promote the integration of students in local schools.

The itinerant teachers' days should be comparably defined so they can provide comprehensive services to their students. Their caseloads should be such that, within the daily total of teaching minutes negotiated for classroom teachers, itinerant teachers can perform these functions: provide direct services (that is, working directly one-on-one with students) or monitoring services (that is, observing students and providing consultative services) as specified on students' IEPs; adapt classroom materials for the students' use either directly or in conjunction with a transcriber; consult with classroom teachers; observe students periodically; assess referrals; and travel between sites. Furthermore, itinerant teachers should have a conference-preparation period equal to that of the classroom teachers in the school district. During this period, the itinerant teachers should be able to work in their offices where materials and records are stored so they can more easily prepare for lessons, complete paperwork and write reports, make and receive telephone calls, plan in-service programs, and order materials. In addition, a duty-free lunch break at an appropriate time and at a stationary site (not in the car or otherwise en route) should be scheduled. Comparable working conditions should be available for teachers whose sponsoring agencies, such as county offices of education, may not stipulate working conditions for classroom teachers.

3. *The itinerant teachers in a program are certified in education of visually impaired students.* In addition to utilizing good teaching techniques, the itinerant teachers have a thorough understanding of the social, psychological, and medical implications of visual impairment and the impact of visual impairment on each student's interaction with his or her school, family, and community. They are also knowledgeable about appropriate interventions that will enhance the student's participation in the educational process.

In the hurried complexity of traveling from site to site, effective itinerant teachers keep in mind this goal: to encourage, educate, and allow each student to be an independent, competent, contributing member of society and an advocate on his or her own behalf. They remember to discourage passivity by never doing anything for students that the students can do themselves. The teachers' sense of success and accomplishment comes from knowing that students are able and willing to take responsibility, commensurate with their developmental levels, for their own special needs.

Chapter
3

A Typical Year

A N ITINERANT TEACHER can expect to be involved in certain processes and activities during the school year. The following sections outline these basic activities and offer suggestions for establishing caseloads, providing textbooks, setting up a schedule, providing in-service programs, developing IEPs, arranging for standardized tests, performing other special activities, and completing end-of-the-year activities. The activities are described in roughly the same chronological order that they present themselves to a teacher's attention during the school year, but this order will vary according to individual experience. Setting up caseloads and ordering textbooks are two substantial items that are best taken care of before a new year begins in the fall.

ESTABLISHING CASELOADS

In a district with only one itinerant teacher, the caseload is predetermined. In larger programs, students should be assigned to teachers in May or June of the previous year to expedite the provision of services in the fall.

The itinerant teachers in a program can be responsible as a group for establishing their caseloads for the coming year. However, if the administrator for the program is involved in the process of assigning caseloads, the teachers can provide important information regarding the students' needs. Some of the factors that should be considered for each student are these: the number of minutes for direct contact or monitoring needed each week, the amount of time needed to obtain or prepare materials, and the length of time the student has been with a particular itinerant teacher. Another important factor is time required to do the following: consult with school personnel, observe students, assess referrals, travel between sites, and have conference-preparation and lunch periods. Because administrators may not be aware of all the demands and nuances involved in an itinerant position, involving the teachers in the process of establishing caseloads may well generate more cohesive, effective services to the students.

Dividing students among itinerant teachers can be accomplished by using different approaches, such as the following ones:

Print and braille versions of work done at the computer. Time to focus on individual needs and abilities is affected by a teacher's caseload size.

Setting up Caseloads

■ *Geographic approach.* In the geographic approach, the area served is divided into as many parts as there are itinerant teachers, in such a way that each teacher has an equitable caseload. This approach works best in a huge geographic area and reduces the itinerant teachers' travel time, which allows for more contact time in each school. However, using this approach may make it difficult to achieve balanced caseloads of students in regard to age levels, types or degrees of visual impairment, and individual needs.

■ *Specific-level approach.* In the specific-level approach, itinerant teachers may specialize in elementary, secondary, or special-class students. This approach reduces the number of materials with which the teachers need to be familiar. However, there are disadvantages to this approach: each secondary school student will have more teachers with whom the itinerant teacher will need to consult (five or six per student as opposed to the usual one per elementary student), and secondary school students are more difficult to schedule for contact time with their itinerant teachers because of their more rigid class schedules.

■ *Eclectic approach.* In the eclectic approach, students are assigned to teachers according to severity of their visual impairment, estimated need in hours, heterogeneity of grade level, and class assignment. Each teacher has some secondary, some elementary, and some special-class students, as well as some continuing students and some new students, some students who require much attention, and some students who need only monitoring. Using this approach is possible in areas in which mileage is not an inhibiting factor.

Whenever possible, it is advisable to assign only one itinerant teacher to each site where there are students. Doing so reduces confusion in the schools and is a more effective use of the itinerant teachers' time.

Becoming familiar with a student's visual, academic, and social functioning takes some time on an itinerant basis, so a teacher should be assigned to a student for more than one year. However, working with the same teacher on a one-to-one basis for several years can foster a student's undue dependence on the teacher. In a district with more than one itinerant teacher, students' progress may be enhanced by rotating the itinerant teachers every three years or so. It is helpful to the students, parents, and school personnel if important suggestions are reiterated by more than one teacher. It is also probable that a new teacher's fresh approach may generate progress. But it is judicious to avoid transferring a student from one itinerant teacher to another when the student is making another type of transition, such as moving from an elementary school to a junior high school.

PROVIDING TEXTBOOKS

If you are a new itinerant teacher for visually impaired students for whom textbooks have not been ordered, determine which students need adapted materials and contact the students' classroom teachers to get lists of the textbooks being used. It is advisable to complete this task as quickly as possible because books may not be delivered until two to six weeks after they have been ordered.

Whenever possible, order textbooks during the spring before any given school year. Two months before the end of school, begin gathering lists of books your students will be using for the following year. Books can then be ordered in June or brailled, enlarged, or taped over the summer and be available for use in September. Be sure to get complete information about each book (full title, author, publisher, and latest copyright date listed) to expedite ordering.

It is usually easy to obtain lists of textbooks at elementary schools. Confer with each principal to determine which teacher or teachers will provide the information. Secondary schools are more of a challenge because not every teacher uses the same texts. After you obtain the list of courses for the next year for each student, check with the textbook clerk for information about the textbooks. If the clerk is not certain about a textbook for a particular class, you may find it necessary to ask an administrator to have your student assigned to a particular teacher and then to contact the teacher to determine which books will be used.

The sample book order form shown on page 13 may serve as a guide concerning the information you should obtain. Be sure to give teachers or clerks enough time to complete the forms, but clearly state deadlines and how they should return the forms to you.

When you have the information you need, check all the sources that may be able to provide the texts. Companies and agencies that provide texts in braille or large print or on tape are listed in Appendix A. You might also be able to obtain adapted books from state or local agencies or volunteer groups. If you are unfamiliar with such agencies or groups, your colleagues in the program for visually impaired students are good sources of information. The organizations listed in Appendix B are useful sources of information as well.

In obtaining texts, try to make decisions judiciously about purchasing or borrowing books or ordering them on tape. For example, if you have the option of borrowing any adapted texts, do so if the braille is transcribed accurately or if the print size is appropriate for a given student's use. Borrowing a textbook is particularly wise if it appears that it will be used only once in your district.

Before ordering textbooks on tape, be sure that your students' listening skills are such that they can benefit from using taped materials. When enlarging books on a copier for a student, be sure you clearly understand the student's visual needs so you produce a print size appropriate for his or her use.

In September, before delivering the books to the schools, check with students' teachers to make sure that the texts you have ordered coincide with the ones that will be used in their classes. It may not be feasible to check with the teachers in all districts, particularly in rural areas, but doing so can reduce the amount of materials you load into and out of your car.

The visually impaired students have to be able to use the texts as independently as possible. Therefore, make certain that page numbers in braille and large-print texts correspond with those of the regular print texts, and check for texts, such as elementary mathematics books and social science textbooks, in which color plays an important role. You may choose to color important areas in enlarged books for students for whom such color will be meaningful so the students have access to the same information as do their classmates.

Work with the classroom teachers and the students, particularly in elementary schools, to organize the volumes in the classroom so the students can easily find the volumes they need. In addition, take time to teach the students how to use books that are published in several volumes.

The students may need to use a special arrangement of desks or tables or both to have ample room to use their special books and equipment. Make sure the seating is arranged so that the students are an integral part of the class and visually impaired students are placed where they can use their vision and optical aids optimally.

The original print size of texts, worksheets, and other materials can vary widely. For students who need large print, if you enlarge all materials by the same proportion, for example, 130 percent, some print may be too small or too large for effective reading. It is wise to assess the correct print size that each student requires for reading each year. You may find it helpful to obtain three measures: the optimal size and the largest and smallest sizes the student will tolerate. Keep records of those sizes by the copier or computer you use most, and also keep them with you in case you need to enlarge materials at another site. Make sure your transcriber, classroom teachers, and parents are also aware of the print sizes that are appropriate for students' efficient reading.

Book Order for September _1990_

Please return this form to _Jean Olmstead_ by _5/25/90_

Please put this form in my mailbox or send it to me at _Central School_
via school mail.

Thanks.

Student _Charles Santos_
Teacher of the Visually Impaired _J. Olmstead_
School _Wright_ Grade _6_
Large Print _✓_ Braille ____

Title _Real Math, Grade 6_ Level _Green_
Author _Willoughby et al_ Publisher _Open Court_
Copyright _1987_

Office Use Only		
Source	Date Ordered	Date Received
In V.I. Program Office		

Title _Our World Today_ Level ____
Author _Bacon_ Publisher _Allyn & Bacon_
Copyright _1986_

Office Use Only		
Source	Date Ordered	Date Received
Available from the State		

Title _Reading Literature_ Level _Grade 6 - Gold_
Author _Chaparro et al_ Publisher _McDougal, Littell_
Copyright ____

Office Use Only		
Source	Date Ordered	Date Received
Amer. Printing House		

A student may have 30 to 40 volumes of books at school. If you enlarge or braille and bind many volumes, the spines and covers may all look the same. Two procedures can facilitate a student's finding a specific volume more quickly:

Labeling Textbooks

■ *Label books consistently.* Choose a format you like, and use it for every volume. For example, if you use the wording in the sample label shown below, your students will realize that the title always comes first; information on the volume, second; and page numbers, third, on both the spines and covers of volumes.

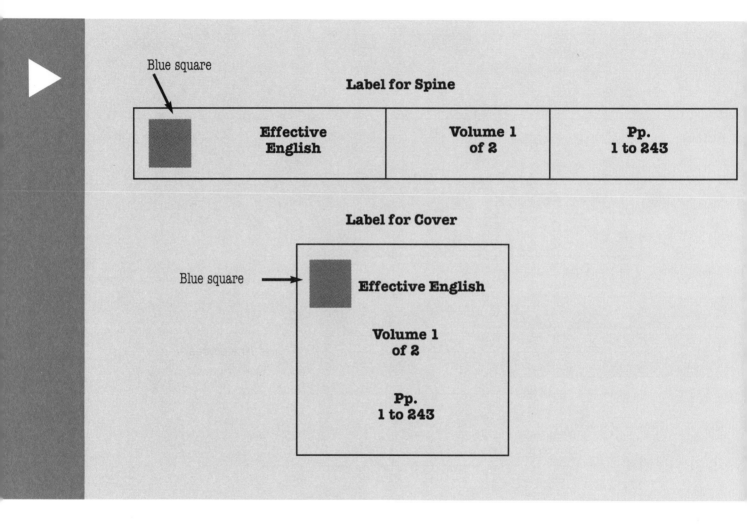

Blue square

Label for Spine

| Effective English | Volume 1 of 2 | Pp. 1 to 243 |

Label for Cover

Blue square

Effective English

Volume 1 of 2

Pp. 1 to 243

■ *Color code labels on large-print books using templates and marking pens.* Always use a particular color and symbol for a particular subject. For example, if mathematics books have red circles, students can locate the volumes with that symbol before reading for specific information. The list on page 15 is a sample of a color-coding system that can be used to designate the subjects of students' books.

If a visually impaired student uses many texts on tape, color coding the tapes by subject area can help the student find the ones he or she needs. You could use the sample system provided here or let the student set up another system.

SAMPLE COLOR-CODING SYSTEM

Red: ●   Mathematics
          ■   Typing

Green: ●   Drama
          ▲   Reading

Purple: ●   History

Orange: ●   Handwriting
          ■   Spelling
          ▲   Computers

Yellow: ●   Health
          ■   Home economics
          ▲   Vocational education
(Outline yellow shapes in black to enhance their visibility.)

Blue: ■   English
          ▲   Music

Brown: ■   Foreign language

Black: ▲   Science

SETTING UP A SCHEDULE

Many itinerant teachers are responsible for establishing their own schedules. The process is complex and time consuming and should be done with care: you generally have to live with your schedule for 10 months.

Time for the following components should appear on your schedule:

■ Direct or monitoring services for students, as specified in their IEPs.

■ Adaptation of materials for students' use and time to confer with the transcriber.

■ Conferences with classroom teachers.

■ Observations of students.

■ Assessment of referrals.

■ Travel between sites.

■ Conference-preparation periods.

■ Lunch breaks.

■ Meetings with other itinerant teachers in your program.

Items for Scheduling

Your goal is to establish your schedule as soon as possible in the fall to provide regular services as soon as possible. Also, because itinerant teachers have to compete for work space with other ''special'' personnel (nurses, speech therapists, psychologists, and so forth), establishing your schedule as early as possible may facilitate your assignment to appropriate working spaces. Schools in some districts have been getting more crowded for a number of reasons, and competition for work space can be fierce.

To begin thinking about your schedule, you must have an approximate idea of how much time each of your students requires, for example, a half hour twice a week or an hour five times a week. To find this out, check the students' IEPs, which will specify the number of contact or monitoring minutes needed. The time required for consulting with parents and teachers and preparing materials should also be considered.

Itinerant teachers with no input from other teachers of visually impaired students will need time to assess their students' needs. Through a review of information about each student's visual functioning and academic progress and observations of students, a new itinerant teacher will gain insight into the students' needs.

Making Preliminary Preparations

Secondary school counselors and their students' schedules are usually available at schools two weeks before the school year begins. Start gathering information on schedules for secondary school students at that time because after school begins, the counselors and other staff are inundated with schedule changes and new enrollees.

These are the benefits of gathering the information early:

Benefits of Early Planning

■ You can be sure that your students are assigned to appropriate courses. A helpful counselor will also facilitate your students' assignment to classroom teachers whose classes are structured to promote the students' integration.

■ With the counselor's assistance, you can manipulate students' schedules to counteract eye fatigue and strain. You may alternate classes that involve many visual tasks with those that emphasize less precise visual learning or, for students who experience eye fatigue in the afternoon, schedule classes with more visual tasks in the morning.

■ You can check all your secondary school students' schedules for appropriate pull-out times when they are to work with you. If three students at three different schools have pull-out periods at the same time, changing their schedules will facilitate your scheduling. Also, if you have two students at one school, you can schedule their pull-out classes back to back so you can see them one after the other and hence avoid using your time inefficiently. If a student's schedule needs to be changed, it is easier for all concerned if the change is made before school begins.

■ If you plan to have a class with a student, that is, see the student every day, you can schedule that class. Seeing a student for a period every day is beneficial for those students who need more support. A school administrator will help you devise a title for the course and show you how to report attendance and grades.

■ You can prepare handouts for the classroom teachers in which you discuss your students' needs and ask for information and put them in the teachers' mailboxes before school begins. (Samples are in the section, "Providing In-service Programs," in this chapter.) The teachers will then have advance notice that a visually impaired student will be in their class, and they can give you helpful information before they are inundated with students and a myriad of organizational chores.

■ You may be able to request your workroom for certain periods before school begins. Being able to set up your workroom at the beginning of the year gives you a head start in providing services to the students at that site.

Scheduling Students

You need to look at your students' needs as you begin to think about your schedule. If you have an elementary school student who requires daily contact of an hour or more, consult with the student's classroom teacher about appropriate times to see the student. Otherwise, it is usually advisable to schedule secondary school students before you schedule your elementary school students, since secondary school schedules are usually more rigid because of the structure of the class periods. Next, find out the times when elementary school and special-class students will be available. This process is not linear. Keep notes of when each student can be seen on which days, and juggle the times on your schedule as they seem to fit best for both the students and the most effective use of your time. For example, give students who tend to experience eye fatigue in the afternoon a slot in your schedule later in the day, when you have more control over the visual tasks to be performed. Also, since most school holidays are on Mondays and Fridays, it is wise to avoid those days for scheduling students you see once a week.

Scheduling students before or after school or during lunch, when possible, allows them to participate fully in their regular classes. However, such a schedule is, of course, difficult to arrange for every student, so arrangements have to be made to pull at least some of the students out of their classes. Make a clear arrangement with each teacher involved about whether the students will be responsible for the time they miss in class and, if so, how they should make that time up.

Try to see students during times when making up the work they miss is not a major problem. The content of the class missed and the teacher's flexibility will affect your decision. A physical education teacher may be willing to excuse a secondary school student from class, but only once per week; therefore, you may need to arrange to see the student during another period, such as home economics or art, if you are to see the student twice a week. Be diplomatic with other teachers during negotiations about scheduling, and understand the importance of each class; at the same time, be assertive enough to schedule students as often as is necessary to provide effective services.

While you are conferring with teachers, keep in touch with school administrators to make sure rooms are available at the times you can see your students. You may need to make several adjustments before you can arrange a workable schedule.

Also, during this scheduling process, check with your students' teachers to make sure they are using the texts you have ordered, deliver books and equipment to the schools and students' homes, and transcribe dittos. This can be a trying time; be calm and flexible, and cooperate with everyone for the benefit of your students. Do not be surprised or upset if the process takes at least three weeks. Take heart; establishing a schedule becomes easier the more you do it.

When your schedule is firmly set, confirm pull-out times with the teachers involved. Usually, the wisest use of time results when secondary school students report directly to you, rather than checking in with their regular teachers first. Set up a way to handle the reporting of attendance. You can ask the regular teacher not to mark a student absent on the days you see him or her, and arrange to be responsible for informing the teacher and the attendance office when the student is not present. If the teacher inadvertently marks the student absent when the student is with you, it should be easy to clear those absences with the teacher and the attendance clerk.

Finally, you can ask the counselors of your secondary school students to avoid making changes later in the school year in the students' schedules that would affect your scheduled time with the students. With the counselors' permission, you can leave a note on their copies of the students' schedules reminding the counselors to call you if a change in schedule is being considered.

Scheduling Other Components

After you have set up times to work with your students, there should be adequate time left in your schedule for the following:

Completing a Schedule

- ◼ *Adaptation of materials.* Providing adapted materials for students on a daily basis is an essential part of your job. Schedule time to consult with your transcriber or to braille, tape, or enlarge the materials necessary to facilitate the students' participation in class activities. Even if a transcriber adapts most of the materials, you may need some time for last-minute work that needs to be adapted immediately.

- ◼ *Observations and consultation.* In effective programs for visually impaired students, itinerant teachers have adequate time to observe students at different points during the year and to consult regularly with their classroom teachers. The observations and exchange of information enable you and the teachers to assist the students according to their needs and capabilities.

- ◼ *Assessment of referrals.* Often, one of the duties of an itinerant teacher is to perform functional vision assessments for referrals to the program for visually impaired students. Adequate time for this function should also be included in your schedule.

- ◼ *Travel time.* Allocate enough time not only to travel safely between schools but to park, walk in, sign in, and get to your room at least a few minutes before your student arrives.

- ◼ *Conference-preparation periods.* Each itinerant teacher should have a daily conference-preparation period scheduled at the office in which the materials and records for visually impaired students are stored. During this period, you can prepare for your lessons with students, gather or prepare the materials to be used in the lessons, and perform other tasks, such as writing reports, ordering materials, completing paperwork, planning in-service activities, and receiving and making telephone calls. Because your access to the office is probably limited, you will find it helpful to schedule at least one preparation period at the end of the day so you can stay late to catch up with work.

Time	Monday	Tuesday	Wednesday	Thursday	Friday
8:00	Davis / George G.	Referrals, Teacher Conference, or Student Observation	Spenser / Conferences and Materials Preparation	Davis / George G.	Westerly / Mary L.
8:30					
9:00	Travel	Travel	Travel	Travel	Travel
9:30	Office / Preparation Period	Grant / Joan G. / David J. / Michael O.	Southport / Kathy D.	Southport / Kathy D.	Grant / Joan G. / David J. / Michael O.
10:00	Travel		Travel / Referrals, Teacher Conference, or Student Observation / Travel	Travel	
10:30	Spenser / Paul W.		Davis / George G.	Spenser / Paul W. / Ellen J.	Travel
11:00					Office
11:30	Lunch	Lunch	Lunch	Lunch	Lunch
12:00	Teacher Conference Materials Preparation	Teacher Conference	Teacher Conference	John M.	Preparation Period
12:30	Travel	Travel	Travel	Travel	Travel
1:00	Southport / Kathy D.	Westerly / Mary L.	Office / Preparation Period	Office / Preparation Period	Referrals, Teacher Conference, or Student Observation
1:30	Travel / Referrals, Teacher Conference, or Student Observation / Travel				
2:00	Travel	Travel	Travel		Travel
2:30	Spenser / Linda S. →	Office / Preparation Period	Spenser / Linda S. →	VI Meeting →	Spenser / Linda S. →
3:00					
3:30					

Notes

Davis — George Gonzalez

Spenser — Ellen Jackson, John Martinez, Linda Smith, Paul Wong

Southport — Kathy Doe

Westerly — Mary Lee

Grant — Joan Grady, David Jones, Michael O'Brien

Note: Dotted lines separate different activities at the same site.

■ *Lunch breaks.* You should be able to schedule a lunch break at an appropriate time of the day. You will often find that you have the best rapport and relationships with regular teachers in schools where you eat lunch. Scheduling lunch at different schools during the week will broaden your base of communication. The best use of time is to schedule a student before or after the lunch period, if possible, on the days you eat lunch at the site.

■ *Meetings with other itinerant teachers in your program.* Meeting regularly with the other itinerant teachers in the program results in more cohesive provision of services to the visually impaired students. It is helpful to schedule such meetings at the end of one day so issues can be discussed thoroughly. (See the sample schedule on page 19 for an idea of how all these components fit in a schedule.)

PROVIDING IN-SERVICE PROGRAMS

Teachers in regular classrooms who have visually impaired students in their classes need practical information so they can help make effective adaptations. Providing information and suggestions for regular teachers is one of the more important roles of the itinerant teacher because it expedites the participation of visually impaired students in school activities.

You can discuss the special needs of the visually impaired students in formal in-service programs and in informal meetings with school personnel. The informal discussions are equally as important as the formally arranged meetings.

On-site meetings with groups of classroom teachers should be arranged with a site administrator who will either ask the teachers to the meeting or ask you to invite them. At sites where only one classroom teacher is involved with the visually impaired student, confer with that teacher to schedule a time when you can meet to discuss mutual concerns. The supervisor of the program for visually impaired students should be involved in arrangements for general in-service programs to which teachers from different sites are invited.

Plan your in-service activities thoroughly. Coining short phrases helps teachers remember key issues. For example, you could use "The helping hand strikes again" when discussing overprotection or doing too much for students.

Many teachers have never had a visually impaired student in their classes. Be prepared to respond to questions and concerns and to deal with a wide range of attitudes. Sometimes it is effective to invite the previous year's regular classroom teachers to in-service discussions and have them share their experiences with students' new teachers.

You may find it advisable to negotiate with your supervisor about reimbursing teachers' attendance at formal, lengthy in-service programs and establishing a budget code for reimbursement. Even nominal payment can help to alleviate feelings of being overburdened. When a lengthy in-service program for a classroom teacher is indicated, it is a good idea to use the district's or program's money to pay for a half-day substitute for the teacher so intervention techniques can be thoroughly discussed.

Participation of Students

When students are involved in an in-service activity, they become doers rather than "done to'ers." They also gain experience and confidence in talking about the implications of their visual impairments. Teachers may be more responsive and empathic if the students are present. Also, they will sometimes ask questions only the students can answer.

The students' ages and levels of functioning will influence the extent of their participation. For example, some five year olds could be involved as "consultants" in planning, demonstrate equipment or techniques, and name three games they like to play. Older elementary school students can assume a more involved role in planning and presenting information about their visual functioning.

Junior high school students can prepare for an in-service program by writing or typing a report that includes the following: visual condition and explanation, corrected acuity and its functional significance, school activities for which they need no assistance, activities and tasks that require remediation, how regular teachers can help them, and what the itinerant teacher does for them. When students have been involved in the process for a number of years, by the time they are in high school, they can assume the major role in presenting in-service programs and writing letters to teachers about their needs. Although students' participation is mentioned sparingly in the following descriptions of in-service activities, your students will benefit from being included in every aspect as much as possible.

In-service Activities for Teachers Whose Students Work with Braille

Although a meeting early in the year with the classroom teachers of any visually impaired student is essential, meeting at the earliest opportunity with the teachers of students who work with braille is crucial. It is helpful to meet with classroom teachers in the spring before the upcoming school term or before school starts in the fall. On the secondary school level, try to arrange one meeting for all the teachers. Before the meeting, you may wish to distribute a letter similar to the sample presented on page 22, in which you describe the reading and writing formats of your visually impaired student and provide other preliminary information. You need to make certain that the texts you ordered in braille or on tape correspond to the ones that will be used in class. Make arrangements for classroom seating that allows the student to be an integral member of the class and to have enough desk space for effective use of materials. Other areas for discussion include the following:

Discussion Topics

- ■ An explanation of the student's visual condition.
- ■ A description of the student's visual acuity.
- ■ A description of the impact of the visual condition on the student's visual functioning (light sensitivity, color recognition, and so on).
- ■ The use of special equipment (computer, braillewriter, slate and stylus, tape recorder, and so forth).
- ■ The use of braille or taped texts. (Explain that braille texts correspond to regular texts—word for word and page for page—and how pictures, graphs, maps, and the like are handled.)
- ■ The use of worksheets or dittos in braille or on tape.
- ■ The process the student will use to complete assigned work (for example, brailled work will be interlined, or the student will type, tape, or do assignments on a computer).

- The role of an aide if one is provided.

- Arrangements for occasions when materials have not been adapted (for example, an aide or peer reads the material to the student or the student does alternative work).

- Expectations about the student's work (for instance, some lessons may be modified, but generally the student should be expected to perform the same tasks as do regular students and should be graded according to the quality of his or her work).

- Expectations about social behavior (for instance, behavior should be appropriate for the setting; ''eye'' contact should be encouraged).

- Extra time that the student may need to complete the work in braille.

- The need to verbalize and explain in more detail activities and boardwork.

- The role of the itinerant teacher.

- The role of the O&M specialist, who may demonstrate and discuss travel techniques.

- Arrangements for getting materials or worksheets in braille or on tape.

August 30, 1990

Kathy Ellis, who uses braille to read and write, is enrolled in your _4th period math_ class. I have been planning extensively to facilitate her participation in your class.

I look forward to meeting you and her other teachers on Tuesday, September 2, at 1:30 P.M. in Room 202 as previously planned. Please put the following items in my mailbox before then or bring them to the meeting:

1. A list of the texts you will be using this year with the following information: title, author, publisher, and copyright date.

2. The masters of any dittos or handouts you have already prepared for her class. Please write on each your name and the approximate date you expect to use it in class.

3. Any work you have planned to put on the board.

4. A list of anything else you can think of that Kathy will need for your class.

I will answer any questions you may have at the meeting and look forward to working with you this year.

Sincerely,

Jean Olmstead

Jean Olmstead
Itinerant Teacher, Visually Impaired
320-4500

September 2, 1990

Re: Kathy Ellis

Any work to be brailled for Kathy should be put in my mailbox with <u>your name and the date you will use it in class</u>. Please give it to me at least two days before you plan to use it. Assigning a responsible classmate to assist Kathy with work that is not brailled would be helpful.

Kathy will braille her work and give it to you. Put it in my mailbox, and I will interline (i.e., write out line for line) exactly what she has brailled and return it to you for grading.

Please contact me if problems arise. I will work with Kathy during the third period daily and can assist her as she needs help.

Helpful Hints

1. There's little need to change your vocabulary. The use of words such as "look," "see," and "watch" is appropriate.

2. Verbalize, verbalize, verbalize. This is important because Kathy cannot see everything your sighted students can. Some teachers find it helpful to pretend they are doing a radio program.

3. Please be considerate as well as practical with Kathy's seating arrangements.

4. Standards for appropriate behavior are just as important for Kathy as for any other student.

Thanks for your cooperation. I'm available during lunch on Thursdays and after school on Mondays and Wednesdays for conferences. Leave a note in my mailbox if you need to talk with me.

Sincerely,

Jean Olmstead

Jean Olmstead
Itinerant Teacher, Visually Impaired
320-4500

■ Arrangements for the times when it is appropriate for the itinerant teacher to work with the student.

You will present a lot of information for teachers to absorb, particularly if they have never taught a visually impaired student. You may find it helpful to provide some of the information in written form (see sample letter above). It is more important, however, to be available throughout the school year for offering consultation, answering questions, and providing reinforcement, either informally in the faculty room or formally in scheduled meetings. Making your availability known informally and formally is advisable too.

You may find it valuable to conduct an in-service program for the entire faculty, particularly if a school has never before had a student who reads in braille. You can present more general information and demonstrate some equipment, adapted materials, and techniques. Showing a film, such as *What Do You Do When You See a Blind Person?* can also be effective. (For information on this film, you can contact the American Foundation for the Blind, listed in Appendix B.)

Classified personnel and administrators also need information about dealing with a blind or visually impaired person. Give helpful suggestions to administrators, counselors, secretaries, clerks, yard supervisors, custodians, cafeteria workers, and bus drivers.

In-service Activities for Teachers Whose Students Read Print

For students in secondary school who read print, you may choose to put a letter similar to the sample presented below in teachers' mailboxes before school starts so they will know that they will have a visually impaired student in their classes. Copies of the letter should be distributed also to principals, vice principals, nurses, counselors, and other adults who will be involved with the student. If some time will elapse between your distribution of the letter and your meeting the staff, you can attach a copy of your photograph to the letter to make it easier for teachers to recognize and find you.

August 28, 1990

Dear _____ Mrs. Jones _____,

Paul Ritter, who is enrolled in your _____ 1st period English _____ class, is visually impaired. He is an albino whose eyes and skin are particularly sensitive to light.

Paul needs

— <u>Preferential seating</u>. He should not have to face bright lights or windows. A front row seat is best for him in most situations.

— <u>Black-on-white copies of handouts</u>. His reading speed and accuracy will increase if you give him a Xeroxed copy of your ditto master.

— <u>Large-print texts</u>. Some large-print books have been ordered for Paul's use. To help me deliver the texts, please complete the attached sheet.

I will be working with you and Paul this year to provide appropriate materials and adaptations to facilitate his participation in class activities. I will contact you again soon. If you have questions in the interim, you can put a note in my mailbox or call my office.

Sincerely,

Jean Olmstead

Jean Olmstead
Itinerant Teacher, Visually Impaired
320-4500

To _Mrs. Jones_

Please complete this questionnaire and put it in my mailbox by _4th period, Sept. 7_.

Thank you,

Jean Olmstead

Jean Olmstead
Itinerant Teacher, Visually Impaired

1. Texts to be used in class:

Title	Author	Publisher	Copyright Date	Dates Used
Eng. Grammar + Comp.	Warriner + Griffith	Harcourt Brace Jovanovich	1973	1st Sem.
Focus on Lit.: Viewpoints	McFarland et al	Houghton Mifflin	1981	2nd Sem.
Animal Farm	Orwell			October

2. I use { no / ~~some~~ / many } dittos. (That is, work written in purple letters.)

_No_ 3. My worksheets sometimes involve print smaller than the size used here.

Yes 4. I use the chalkboards, overhead projector, or films at least three times a week.

Yes 5. I would like to learn how to enlarge worksheets using the office copier.

6. The best time to confer with me is

Day of week _Tuesday_

Time/Period _Third_

Location _Room 101_

The teachers' completion of a questionnaire similar to the one presented above, which should accompany the letter you send, can give you crucial information. Be clear about when their responses should be in your mailbox. A second letter like the one on page 26 can be given to pertinent personnel when you have established your schedule at the school.

Letters are helpful but do not take the place of face-to-face meetings. In the case of a secondary school student, confer with the school administrator regarding a group meeting at the beginning of the year with all your student's teachers. The administrator may suggest that you meet individually with each teacher during a conference period; however, a brief meeting after school is a more efficient use of your time. Also, meeting in a group may stimulate discussion of common concerns.

September 30, 1990

To teachers of the following visually impaired students:

George Harmon   Ann Sawyer   Susan Gifford   Kevin Smith

I now have a schedule at Belmont:

Monday:	Period 3 Kevin
	Period 7 Ann
Wednesday:	Period 7 Ann
Thursday:	Period 3 Kevin
	Period 4 George
	Period 5 Susan
Friday:	Period 7 Ann

I plan to be available for conferences regarding these students' participation in your class during lunch on Mondays or after school. Please contact me if your student experiences visual or academic difficulties in your class.

I have brought large-print copies of the <u>New World Dictionary</u> and <u>Roget's Thesaurus</u> to the library here. Please leave a note for me if your student will need to use an encyclopedia for research. I have a large-print copy that I could also put in the library.

Each of these students will benefit if you will provide materials, particularly worksheets, that have good contrast. For George, Susan, and Kevin, please make size-for-size copies of your ditto masters if the original print is no smaller than this. If your print is smaller than pica, please enlarge the worksheets slightly.

Ann's worksheets need to be enlarged 154 percent. I have put 11" x 17" paper in the paper tray of the main office copier for this purpose. Additional paper is stored in the phone room next to the nurse's room. When you enlarge material on the 11" x 17" paper, please trim pages to a manageable size and staple them.

If you want me to enlarge or copy worksheets for you, put the masters in my mailbox and include your <u>name and the date you will use them in class</u>. Check my Belmont schedule to make sure I'll be there in time to enlarge the work.

I've appreciated your cooperation in returning forms to me. I look forward to working with you this year.

Sincerely,

Jean Olmstead

Jean Olmstead
Itinerant Teacher,
Visually Impaired
320-4500

At the meeting, emphasize the fact that the classroom teachers are responsible for the visually impaired student just as they are responsible for other students in the class and that your role is to provide materials, instruction, and suggestions for techniques that will facilitate the visually impaired student's participation in class activities. Discuss the student's visual condition and its implications, the student's strengths, what intervention techniques will enhance the student's participation in class, and what services you will provide. If the teachers have already received written information from you, reiterate your schedule at the school, procedures for contacting you, and procedures for getting materials in large print. Ask the teachers to inform you if any problems that seem to be related to the student's visual impairment arise.

For elementary school students, individual conferences may be arranged with each teacher, emphasizing the same information. In some school districts, teachers have a workday before students report for school in the fall. You may arrange for a brief meeting on that day to introduce yourself, describe your student's special needs and intervention techniques, and deliver materials and equipment. A conference during which you and your student provide more detailed information can be arranged later.

General In-service Programs

As a group, the itinerant teachers in a district may choose to present a more elaborate in-service program for classroom teachers, administrators, and support staff who are involved with visually impaired students. You may be able to reimburse teachers for their attendance or include supper to encourage their participation.

If possible, schedule the meeting at a site where much of your adaptive equipment and materials are located. Present general information regarding visual impairments and their impact on people's lives. More specifically, you can give the teachers eyeglasses that simulate their visually impaired students' visual conditions and then have them participate in activities that involve reading smudged blackboards, faint dittos on colored paper, and small print and performing physical education and daily living tasks. Display equipment and aids, such as lamps; reading-writing stands; video magnifiers, or closed-circuit televisions (CCTVs); magnifiers; and large-print and braille materials. Two or three visually impaired students can describe their experiences and feelings. In addition, you can discuss the role of the itinerant teacher.

Presenting such an in-service program is a major project, but it is well worth the effort. Keeping good records of organizational details from year to year eases the preparation.

Generally, classroom teachers who attend an in-service program are more understanding of their students' needs, more responsible about providing materials for transcribing, and more open to suggestions. They also may develop a heightened awareness of visual disabilities, which may generate more referrals to your program.

Other In-service Arrangements
The Student's Classmates

Another type of in-service program can be provided to the visually impaired student's classmates (particularly at the elementary school level), who may be curious about the special materials in the classroom. Gear the program to the academic level of the class, and involve your student in the presentation—according to his or her abilities—to give the student experience and expertise in talking about his or her visual needs. The presentation may include a description of how the eye works, information about how the student's eye works differently, an explanation and a demonstration of adaptive materials and techniques, suggestions for how the class members can be helpful, discussion of what the itinerant teacher and the student work on together, and time for questions.

The Student's Family

Sharing pertinent information with the student's family is also important. Family members need to understand the implications of the student's visual condition, be aware of the materials and techniques used at school, and encourage the use of adaptations and special materials in all aspects of the student's life. You can discuss information during telephone calls or home visits, at the IEP meeting, or at formally arranged meetings with the student's family.

Community Groups

The suggestions presented for in-service programs for other groups will assist you in presenting programs to interested community groups and organizations, such as parent-teacher associations and the local Lions Club. Showing a videotape or slides of different aspects of your program can enhance your presentation.

DEVELOPING INDIVIDUALIZED EDUCATION PROGRAMS (IEPs)

An IEP for every visually impaired student is mandated by the Education for All Handicapped Children Act (P.L.94-142). It is the document that clearly delineates the type and amount of services your students will receive.

In the case of students for whom you provide the only special education service, you are responsible for assessing the students' needs and abilities, writing the IEP, and arranging for and leading the IEP meeting. In the case of students who receive services from more than one special education teacher, the teachers responsible for what is considered the students' main disabling condition assume these duties, with input from the other special education teachers involved with the students. In these instances, your role is to provide pertinent information concerning areas that relate to and are affected by the students' visual conditions, write goals and objectives, and attend the IEP meeting.

IEP meetings should be scheduled at a time when the students' parents will be able to attend. A special education administrator or on-site administrator should also attend the meetings. The students' classroom teachers should be invited, and the students should be present when their participation is appropriate.

Each district has its own requirements and deadlines for IEP conferences. If your conferences are scheduled for November, begin your assessments as soon as school starts; compiling data takes time.

To expedite the process, establish priorities among the areas to be assessed, using information from previous IEPs, observations, and input from teachers. Focus on the students' immediate needs and functional levels.

Set goals realistically. Remember that the classroom teachers are responsible for the bulk of your students' instruction and that your role is to provide services related to the students' needs that result from their visual impairments. Sharing the results of your assessments with the teachers can help them provide appropriate activities and instruction for the visually impaired students.

The following list of sample annual goals and the short-term objectives relating to them is presented to assist you in writing your own:

Sample IEP Goals

Goal: The student will receive adaptive materials and aids and instruction in their use.

Objectives: The student will

1. Use the following equipment at school or at home when appropriate: large-print books, reading/writing stand, enlarged and darkened dittos, felt-tip pens, dome magnifier, monocular, and video magnifier.

2. Locate information in a 12-volume thesaurus, a 24-volume dictionary, and a 30-volume encyclopedia (or a 7-volume math book).

3. Operate a video magnifier independently for reading and writing.

4. Demonstrate the ability to enlarge materials on a copier.

Goal: The student will take standardized tests under appropriate conditions.

Objective: The student will take standardized tests in large print (or braille or on tape) with extended time, and the teacher will mark the student's answer sheet. (List tests, such as the Preliminary Scholastic Aptitude Test [PSAT] or the Scholastic Aptitude Test [SAT], and specify extended time as 1½ times for large print or 2 times for braille.)

Goal: The student will describe and demonstrate exercises for overcoming neck, shoulder, and back tension.

Objectives: The student will

1. Lock his or her fingers in front, straighten the arms, and lift the arms over his or her head as far as possible to the back.

2. Learn tense-relax techniques for relaxing the neck, shoulders, and back.

Goal: The student will demonstrate the best position of light sources for his or her vision.

Objectives: The student will

1. Position a light source behind his or her left shoulder and to the left of the left shoulder when reading and writing.

2. Position natural light behind him or her, and turn to avoid glare when possible.

Goal: The student will demonstrate the proper care of eyeglasses.

Objectives: The student will

1. Clean the eyeglasses with an appropriate amount of solution, using the cleaning cloth correctly.

2. Demonstrate the proper way to lay eyeglasses down on a surface.

Goal: The student's visual functioning will be assessed.

Objective: The student will cooperate and assist in an assessment of his or her visual acuity, visual field, color vision, and general visual functioning.

Goal: The student will demonstrate knowledge of the structure and function of the eye.

Objectives: The student will:

1. Identify the major parts of the eye on a model with _____ accuracy.

2. Describe the basic functions of the parts of the eye with _____ accuracy.

3. Describe the difference between a normally functioning eye and his or her eye, stating which parts are affected and how the differences affect his or her visual functioning.

Goal: The student will demonstrate knowledge of his or her visual condition.

Objectives: The student will

1. Describe his or her visual condition and explain its implications.

2. Describe his or her visual acuity and its implications.

3. Demonstrate or list _____ ways to improve his or her visual functioning.

Goal: The student will communicate his or her visual needs.

Objectives: The student will

1. Participate in role-playing activities in which the student describes his or her visual needs to a friend, teacher, or stranger.

2. Inform an appropriate person when he or she cannot see something.

3. Prepare and present a talk about his or her visual condition and its implications to classmates (or a group of teachers).

4. Ask for materials to be enlarged as needed.

Goal: The student will use adaptations to his or her environment.

Objective: The student will make appropriate changes in the environment to enhance his or her visual functioning (for example, use a magnifier or move to reduce glare or to be able to see the chalkboard).

Goal: The student will demonstrate knowledge of eye care.

Objectives: The student will

1. Describe the roles of an ophthalmologist, an optometrist, and an optician.

2. Describe a typical eye examination.

3. List pertinent information to give to and questions to ask an ophthalmologist or optometrist.

4. Demonstrate the ability to interpret data on an eye report.

5. Maintain records of his or her eye care.

Goal: The student will benefit from assistance for transition from high school.

Objectives: The student will

1. Enroll with the state department of rehabilitation and list _____ ways the department can assist him or her.

2. Begin a personal file of important information: telephone numbers and addresses of agencies, resources, and the like.

3. Obtain information about services for visually impaired persons at _____ colleges.

At the IEP meeting, the amount of time required to provide services to the visually impaired student will be determined and documented on the IEP form. The amount of time and the type of services provided will vary according to the assessed needs of the student and should reflect the time required to achieve the goals agreed on by the IEP team.

Some visually impaired students may require only minimal intervention, and monitoring services may be specified for periods such as 60 minutes a month or even as little as 20 minutes a quarter. Monitoring students entails utilizing the specified time to observe the students in different activities and to consult with school personnel, the students' families, and community resources regarding the students' special needs.

Other students will need direct contact with the itinerant teacher. The time required to achieve the IEP goals can vary from 45 minutes a quarter to two or more hours every day. For these students, it is advisable to specify minutes for consultation on the IEP in addition to the minutes specified for direct services. The number of minutes for consultation should reflect the time needed to adapt class materials and to consult with school personnel, the students' families, and community resources, such as ophthalmologists or optometrists. If a transcriber is available to adapt most of the materials, the total minutes for consultation will be less than if you are directly responsible for brailling, enlarging, or taping the materials.

For students who receive other special education services or are enrolled in special classes, coordinate your IEP development and conferences with the teachers involved. In some districts, you may not be required to write the assessment part of the IEP for special-class students. You may use a form, such as the one presented on page 33, to give the special-class teacher information about the students' visual conditions to include in the IEP health section. Also, because this teacher may have to coordinate the IEP conference with many people, you should let him or her know when you will be available for the conference.

In some districts, elementary school teachers are required to have a conference with each parent in the fall. Whenever possible, schedule your IEP conference in conjunction with the meeting about the student's first report card. You will learn more about the student's progress, the teacher will learn about the goals and objectives, and the parent of the visually impaired student will have to attend only one meeting to hear what both of you have to say.

Having all the students' teachers present at the IEP conference may not always be feasible, particularly at the secondary school level. Therefore, the teachers' completion of the form on page 34 can provide important information for those present at the conference.

The requirements of the IEP may have a special implication when a student enters your program in the middle of the year. That is, when a new student begins a special class or resource room program midyear, he or she can be more easily absorbed into the existing structure. But in an itinerant program, adding a student may entail the teacher's traveling to a new site and scheduling additional time for direct instruction or monitoring, adaptation of materials, consultation, and observations. In larger programs, teachers may be able to adjust their schedules as a group so a new student can be absorbed with no disruption of service to other students. However, if the student is entering a program served by one itinerant teacher whose schedule is full, a problem arises.

The members of the IEP team have a mandated responsibility to plan services according to the assessed needs of each student. IEPs should indicate the actual amount of support and instruction required for the student's successful integration in the classroom and attainment of competence in the special skills related to his or her visual impairment, rather than reflect how much time the itinerant teacher has available considering the other demands on the teacher's time. When the needs of students require more time than you have, hiring additional support for the program (such as a part-time itinerant teacher, a transcriber, or an aide) or providing placement in an alternative program for visually impaired students is necessary.

To: __Ms. Collins__

Re: IEP for __Bert Phillips__

Date: __2/27/90__

Here is information that you may want to include in Part 1 of __Bert__'s
IEP:

Surgeries to correct congenital cataracts have been unsuccessful. Bert appears to have light projection (he will look toward a light source). He does not interact visually with people or objects.

I will be writing my own Part 2 and want to be present at the IEP conference. If possible, please consider these preferences when scheduling the conference:

Best times: Wednesdays before 9
            Mondays between 1 and 2

Please avoid Thursdays after 2:30

Out of town at a conference: March 15-18.

If you cannot schedule the conference at my preferred times, I will understand. Please let me know as soon as the IEP date, time, and site have been confirmed.

Thank you,

Jean

Jean Olmstead
Itinerant Teacher,
Visually Impaired
320-4500

To: _Mrs. Smith_

Re: _Ray Grey_

Date: _1/7/90_

An IEP meeting for _Ray Grey_ is scheduled for _Monday, Jan. 17_ at _1:00_
in _Room 209_. I realize it may be difficult for you to

attend but you may wish to give information to _Ray_'s parent(s) about
his/her participation in your class.

Indicate below if you plan to attend the meeting and add pertinent comments. Please return

this form to my mailbox by _10 AM, Monday, Jan. 17_.

Thank you,

Jean Olmstead

Jean Olmstead
Itinerant Teacher, Visually Impaired
320-4500

Sorry I can't be at the meeting.
Roy seems to be a smart kid who
works below his ability. He needs
to stop getting plugged into the
taunting of his peers.
Absences and incomplete
assignments are affecting his grade.
Current grade: D+
Mrs. Grey should contact me for a
conference.

J. Smith

ARRANGING FOR STANDARDIZED TESTS

Arrange to have your district's testing office automatically send you each year a copy of the testing schedule or schedules so you will know when standardized tests will be administered to your students' classes. Consult with appropriate personnel about the tests; your students may be exempt from taking some of them. Follow your state's regulations on exceptions and modifications.

Some mainstreamed visually impaired students can take the tests with their classes without affecting their scores. For others, make arrangements to have the tests available in braille or large print or on tape and provide for extended testing time (generally allow 1½ times the usual time for large print and twice the usual time for braille). When possible, your students should be tested at the same time as their peers. In most instances, the students should not use the answer sheets provided by the district's testing office. They should mark their answers directly on the adapted copy of the test or use a special answer sheet in braille or large print. You or another adult, such as an aide, will need to transfer the responses to the original answer sheet. Any special accommodations should be noted in the students' folders with the scores.

Secondary students may take tests, such as the PSAT or the SAT, that may not be listed on the testing schedule because they are not administered by the district's testing office. At each site, consult with the school's testing coordinator so provisions can be made with the proper agency for your students to be tested.

PERFORMING OTHER SPECIAL ACTIVITIES

Your schedule will need to be interrupted occasionally for certain activities, such as attending IEP conferences and administering standardized tests. Flexibility is a key concept for an itinerant teacher. Adjustments may also need to be made for spending extensive time with a student, conducting home visits, attending eye examinations with students, and going on study trips.

Special Visits to Schools and Homes

You may find it advisable to spend a week or so, usually at the beginning of the school year, in the classrooms of one or more of your students. Your interventions and observations at this time can be inordinately helpful in assisting the students to form good habits regarding the proper use of materials, equipment, and adaptive techniques. You can also model for school personnel appropriate techniques for assisting the students. Your understanding of and involvement in the students' daily activities will enable you to make suggestions and answer questions from a practical viewpoint. Ideally, your interaction with the students should taper off so that at the end of this period, you can withdraw, assured that the students are participating as fully as possible in their classes' activities.

A home visit may be a comfortable way to share observations and information with your students' parents. You may also choose to deliver bulky items, including reading-writing stands, typing stands, or volumes of books that are lent to the students for the year, and so observe the students interacting in their homes.

Eye Examinations

Attending eye examinations with your students and their parents can provide you with important information that is usually not available in written reports. A general rule is to attend at least one regular eye examination and all low vision examinations with each student. During the examinations, take notes, ask questions, and discuss your observations of the students' visual functioning.

Other suggestions regarding your participation are the following:

Tips for Eye Exams

- ■ Tell parents that you wish to be notified when an eye examination is scheduled so you can accompany them or obtain a report.

- ■ Be prepared for a student's eye examination. Collect notes regarding the student's visual functioning, and make a list of questions you may want to ask the eye care specialist.

- ■ Prepare your student for the examination. Explain the purpose and procedures, and elicit his or her cooperation. Guide the student in formulating questions, and help the student to verbalize his or her abilities and needs (definitely essential before a low vision examination).

- ■ Encourage parents to make a list of their concerns.

- ■ Sometimes an audiotape of an examination is helpful for the student and his or her family; be certain to get participants' permission to make a tape.

- ■ Ophthalmologists and optometrists are busy; sometimes it can take weeks to get a written report. If your district uses a standardized eye report form, take it with you to the appointment; most eye care specialists are willing to complete a form on the spot if they are asked to do so.

- ■ Do not hesitate to call an eye care specialist for clarification if you need it, but be sure a signed form for the release of information is in the specialist's file on the student.

- ■ Call or visit the student's home a few days after the appointment to discuss the examination with your student and his or her parents. You may be able to answer their questions or alleviate their concerns.

Study Trips

Often there is only one visually impaired student in each school. Taking the students in the itinerant program on group study trips allows them to get to know each other. When study trips are scheduled frequently (five to seven a year), a healthy sense of camaraderie may develop among the students. In addition, trips may be scheduled for individual students for various reasons, such as exploring a particular job or receiving orientation to a new school.

When the trips are specially arranged with the visually impaired students in mind, they can be of immense value. The needs of your group may lead you to visit community and private organizations, local attractions, companies that employ visually impaired workers, or facilities that serve visually impaired people. You may also choose to schedule group meetings where students can interact with a visually impaired adult who is a positive role model or participate in group counseling or recreational activities.

Caution: Many special activities require transportation. Some itinerant teachers transport students in their own cars. If you decide to do so, make sure you clearly understand your district's insurance coverage and arrangements concerning legal liability while traveling, both inside and outside the district, with students in your car. If you are concerned about the legal ramifications of using your car for this purpose, you should arrange alternative modes of transportation for such trips.

PERFORMING END-OF-THE-YEAR ACTIVITIES

Performing certain activities at the end of the year will be to your benefit and that of your students and will help you prepare for the following school year. Among them are these:

End-of-the-Year Checklist

■ Get lists of textbooks for the coming year, as described in the section "Providing Textbooks."

■ Consult with appropriate school personnel regarding the visually impaired students' placements for the coming year. Elementary school administrators can be helpful in assigning students to teachers whose classroom structures will facilitate mainstreaming. Occasionally, you may be able to manipulate secondary school students' schedules at this time, but generally special arrangements cannot be made until about two weeks before school starts in the fall, when the schools' master schedules are developed.

■ Meet with the other itinerant teachers in the program, and the appropriate administrator if necessary, to determine caseloads for the coming year, as discussed in the section "Establishing Caseloads." If your caseload for the coming year includes students who were not on your caseload for the year that is ending, have conferences with the students' current itinerant teachers to discuss the students' abilities and special needs.

■ During the last month of school, gradually take materials that are not being used to your office. Doing so will reduce the number of items you have to transport during the last days.

■ Allot time during the last two weeks to collect remaining materials and equipment. Some items may be left in the students' homes or at the schools for summer school use. Returning all other materials ensures that they will be available for use during the following year.

■ Some high schools have a special examination schedule. Get the closing bulletins from your secondary schools so you can adjust your schedule accordingly.

■ Allow time to update files and forms so students' records will be organized for the beginning of the next school year.

■ Once again, acknowledge the classroom teachers' efforts on behalf of the visually impaired students. Thank the teachers for their cooperation in getting materials to you to be transcribed and for utilizing adaptive techniques in the classrooms. Recognition of their acceptance and help can foster their willingness to assist other mainstreamed students.

Chapter 4

Facilitating Integration

VISUALLY IMPAIRED STUDENTS who receive assistance from an itinerant teacher are generally enrolled in their own neighborhood schools or bused to other schools with special education classes. They are enrolled in these schools because they can benefit from extensive participation in the schools' activities and have the necessary skills to utilize special materials and techniques to take care of their visual needs when the itinerant teacher is not at the school. The successful integration of the students depends, in part, on the schools' commitment to mainstreaming and the effective intervention of the itinerant teacher. The school has the foremost responsibility for the visually impaired student; you give specialized support by providing individualized instruction, adapted materials, and specialized equipment; consulting with school personnel; and observing the student periodically.

INDIVIDUALIZED INSTRUCTION

The amount of time you spend with a visually impaired student depends on the student's needs. Careful assessment, which includes observation, consultation with school personnel and the family, and the use of checklists and evaluation tools, provides the data for the IEP team to determine the amount of time you will work with the student. You may see one student once a week for 30 minutes and another student for 120 minutes each day.

When and where you see the student depends on the student's schedule and the availability of school facilities. Sometimes working in the classroom is appropriate; in that instance, you will want to recognize that the classroom teacher is in charge and you are there as support for the visually impaired student. This arrangement works best when your lessons dovetail with the class's activities. In other situations, you and the student will work in another room that is assigned by the school administrator.

Your role is to provide instruction in areas related to and affected by the student's visual condition. The content of your lessons depends on the assessed needs of the student in the following areas: concept development and academic skills, communication skills, social-emotional and sensory-motor development, daily living skills, and career and vocational awareness.

Flexibility is an important attribute of the itinerant teacher. You may be prepared to present a specific lesson only to discover that providing instruction in or assistance with a concept or assignment that was introduced in the student's class is more important. If the student requires more on-the-spot instruction than you anticipated, a reassessment is indicated. If the problems seem to be related to or caused by the visual impairment, it is advisable to increase your time with the student or even to consider alternative placement. If the difficulties appear to stem from causes unrelated to vision, the IEP team should consider other sources of extra support in the district.

The need for flexibility also extends into other areas. For example, you may arrive at a school and discover that you had no prior notification about an activity, such as an assembly or special program, scheduled at the time during which you work with your student. If the special activity seems less meaningful to the student than your lesson, you should work with him or her. When the activity is one the student should not miss, you have several options: (1) you can participate in the activity with the student and provide appropriate interventions, such as by describing what is occurring on the stage during an assembly, (2) you can observe from a distance the student's participation in and use of interventions during the activity, (3) you can remain at the school to confer with personnel, check records, make telephone calls, or complete paperwork, or (4) you can drive to another site where work needs to be done.

ADAPTED MATERIALS

Ideally, at the beginning of the year books in braille or large print or on tape will be delivered to the school for the student's use. During the year, however, much additional material needs to be adapted. The student, classroom teacher, and you will need to be creative about devising methods and utilizing resources to enable the student to participate as fully as possible in the class's activities.

An organized classroom teacher may give you work to be adapted before it is used in class. Some textbook series have accompanying worksheets that you can get at the beginning of the year to be brailled, enlarged, or taped. When dittos are to be transcribed, ask the teachers to give you the darkest, clearest copy, so you or the transcriber will be able to retype, braille, or tape the ditto as easily and quickly as possible. If you have access to an enlarging copier, ask the teachers to give you their ditto masters, which you can enlarge for visually impaired students.

The classroom teacher may find it helpful to have the original worksheet clipped to the brailled or enlarged copy. Always write identifying information on a brailled worksheet in case it becomes separated from its print version.

Handouts prepared at the last minute, boardwork, transparencies for overhead projectors, and so forth are more of a challenge that can be met in a variety of ways:

Ways of Preparing Materials

■ You or a transcriber can visit the school the first thing in the morning to transcribe the materials.

■ An aide, older student, or classmate can read the material to the visually impaired student. In some secondary schools, classmates of the student may be hired as note takers for boardwork. Funding to pay note takers may come from a category established for that purpose in the budget for the program for visually impaired students or from other district programs, such as those relating to work experience.

■ The classroom teacher, an aide, or a responsible student can tape the information.

- An enlarging copier at the school can be used to prepare copies of handouts for students. Various people can be responsible for enlarging handouts: the classroom teacher, an aide, another adult, such as the secretary, or the student if he or she is reliable. You should provide paper in appropriate sizes and make sure that whoever does the enlarging is aware of the optimum print size for the student.

- The visually impaired student does not get the material when the class does. Instead, the student does alternative work and completes the assignment at a later time. Make arrangements with the classroom teacher to be sure that appropriate work is provided for such instances.

Providing students with specialized equipment like computers with voice output is a key aspect of an itinerant program.

SPECIALIZED EQUIPMENT

Providing the specialized equipment a student needs is an important part of your job. Sometimes the special devices and equipment for one student will fill your car. You may find it helpful to use a luggage cart when delivering materials. It is wise in some instances, particularly with bulky items, to request assistance from the custodian with a flatbed dolly.

Work with each student to determine which types of devices and equipment best suit his or her needs. You should have enough of the heavier, bulky items, such as reading-writing stands and braillers, so that one can be left at each site where the student will need them: classrooms, your workroom, and the student's home.

Electronic equipment can be of great value to visually impaired students. You will find it advisable to keep abreast of the latest advances in technology and computer hardware and software by attending conferences and receiving brochures and announcements by mail; being knowledgeable about the capabilities of each device allows you to recommend the purchase of equipment that is most suited to the needs of your students. When possible, do business with companies that lend equipment for a trial period so you and your student can determine its effectiveness. Of course, to assist your student, you will need to be familiar with the operation of each device.

Again, be creative about using the school's resources. If an elementary school class has access to a computer, attaching a voice synthesizer may be all a student needs at a particular time. However, additional specialized equipment needs to be purchased at some point and delivered to the site for the student's instruction and use. Once a student is proficient with a device, creativity in locating funding sources will facilitate the purchase of the equipment for the student's use at home.

In elementary schools, the equipment may be left in the classroom. In secondary schools, some equipment may be left in classrooms, such as an English class, where much reading and writing are required. Sometimes a student may carry devices from class to class; in that case, it may be advisable to transport equipment and materials in a suitcase with wheels. It is necessary to find alternative sites for devices that are too large to carry, but such sites will depend on what is available at the school. The room should be either open all day and staffed by an adult or locked but easily accessible with a key. The arrangements need to be flexible enough to allow the student to use the equipment when it is needed.

Having students and their parents sign a contract similar to the sample video magnifier contract presented in this chapter may encourage the responsible use of devices. In the case of secondary school students, you may also choose to write a letter to inform the students' classroom teachers of the arrangement to use the equipment (see the sample letter on page 44). You can also opt to have the teachers complete a questionnaire attached to your letter (see sample on page 44) to determine whether they understand the purpose of and the arrangements for a student's use of the machine.

CONSULTATION WITH SCHOOL PERSONNEL

In-service programs with school personnel at the beginning of the year should be followed by ongoing contact, which will provide invaluable information about students' academic progress and social skills. In addition, you may need to consult with classroom teachers about students' participation in such activities as art, physical education, assemblies, and study trips and to confer with other staff members, including secretaries, recess and yard-duty supervisors, bus drivers, and cafeteria workers. Keeping abreast of students' interactions at school and arranging for needed support when you are not at a school are important. At the same time, you need to remember that the students are served on an itinerant basis because they can adapt to less than ideal situations and can take some responsibility for their own special needs; it is essential to maintain a balance between providing appropriate assistance and smothering the students with excessive attention.

Develop good consultation skills. Keep notes of issues and questions about which you are

Video Magnifier Contract

I understand that using the video magnifier when no adult is present is a privilege granted to me that may be denied if I am not responsible about following these rules:

1. I will remember to turn off the light and make certain the doors are closed and locked each time I leave the room.

2. I will return the key to the secretary each time I leave.

3. I will use the video magnifier according to instructions. If the machine appears to be broken, I will stop using it and leave a note about the problem in the main office.

4. I will not bring anyone else to the room.

5. I will not bring food into the room.

Marsha Kelley	_10-5-90_
Student's Signature	Date
Anne Kelley	_10-5-90_
Parent's Signature	Date
Jean Olmstead	_10/7/90_
Teacher's Signature	Date

concerned for discussion during meetings with school personnel. Keep your remarks succinct. Do not be surprised if you need to reinforce key issues you addressed at the fall in-service program. Be informed of upcoming school events so you and the teachers can discuss, if necessary, students' participation in special activities. Listen for subtle clues and offhand remarks that may indicate areas that require troubleshooting. Equally important is your acknowledgment of the staff's efforts on behalf of students.

Conferring with a number of teachers at several sites can be accomplished in several ways. You may be able to contact teachers in the faculty room at lunchtime, recess, or before or after school. Some teachers prefer that more formal appointments be made to discuss students' progress.

Have teachers of secondary school students complete a form similar to the sample presented on page 45, which will provide pertinent information. Using the form or a comparable checklist can be a time saver because then you need to have conferences only with teachers in whose classes students are experiencing difficulty.

In a hurried day of traveling, it is difficult to find time to spend in the faculty room or other common meeting places, but casual encounters can result in a helpful exchange of informa-

October 9, 1990

To teachers of Dale Mitchell,

A video magnifier is located in Room E for Dale's use. To use this device, one places regular print material under a magnifying camera, and it is displayed enlarged on a screen.

Dale is proficient in the use of the video magnifier and now has my permission to use the machine during your class periods when students are working independently and books or worksheets have not been enlarged for him. At appropriate times, please send him with a hall pass to the main office so he will be able to complete his assignments more easily.

Please make sure that substitute teachers are aware of this arrangement.

Please return the attached slip to me.

I appreciate your cooperation.

Sincerely,

Jean Olmstead

Jean Olmstead
Itinerant Teacher, Visually Impaired
320-4500

Please check the appropriate choices and return this slip to my mailbox by

5th period, Oct. 11th . Thank you.

Jean Olmstead

1. _Dale Mitchell_ will probably leave my class to use the video magnifier:
   ___ never
   ___ rarely
   ___ 2-3 times a week
   ✓ 4-5 times a week

2. ✓ I would like a demonstration of the video magnifier.
   ___ I would not like a demonstration of this device.

3. ✓ Please contact me to answer my questions about this arrangement.

_____Peter Daniels_____
Signature

o: _Mrs. Watson_

e: _Martha Snyder_

ate: _9/15/90_

lease return this questionnaire to me by _4th period, September 24_

_____.

Thank you,

Jean Olmstead

Jean Olmstead
Itinerant Teacher, Visually Impaired
320-4500

. Please evaluate _____Martha_____'s participation in your class.

Very poor.

2. Have you noticed _____Martha_____ having any problems seeing materials, e.g.,
texts, dittos, or boardwork?

(Yes)   No

Specify: _Martha will never be able to operate a sewing machine. She can only do hand sewing. She has tried to thread the hand sewing needle but usually my T.A. threads her needle. I usually put the knot at the end. She can't take out a knot — no motor skills._

3. Would you like me to contact you personally regarding_____Martha_____?

(Yes)   No

If yes, what is a good time for me to contact you?
_7th period in class or
4th or 8th period are my conference periods._

4. Other comments:
_I've talked to Mrs. Snyder but she wants Martha to stay in sewing, but her success will be almost 0 because she needs more help than we can give.
She needs almost a one-one situation._

45

tion. One option is to eat lunch at various schools during the week. At schools where you have more than one student or a student for whom extra consultation is indicated, schedule the students before or after lunch, if possible, so you can be in the faculty room during the lunch break. By being available in the lunchroom, you can establish a closer relationship with the staff, who will have the opportunity to share pertinent information on a spontaneous basis.

OBSERVATIONS OF STUDENTS

Assessment tools and consultation are effective means for judging students' performance. To ensure successful mainstreaming, periodic observation is also essential. Observe the students at different times of the day. Visit their classes during academic periods to see how they are using their materials and equipment when you are not directly involved. Watch them during art and physical education classes, in the playground, and at lunch. These observations will provide invaluable feedback for assessing students' successes, as well as indicating areas that may require further intervention.

Observing students performing chores or studying at home or participating in community programs is also helpful. You may be able to demonstrate or suggest strategies to enhance their use of effective techniques. Overall, periodic ongoing observations enable you to recommend or provide interventions that facilitate the development of the competencies needed by your students to become contributing members of society.

Chapter 5

Organization of Information and Materials

A TEACHER CAN sometimes feel overwhelmed when dealing with the myriad details of information and materials that teaching in an itinerant program involves. Develop a method for organizing the details and deciding on the materials to take with you as you travel. This chapter outlines the basic information and materials you need.

PERTINENT INFORMATION

Basic Information and Materials

- *For each student.* First, middle, and last names; birthdate; address; telephone number; parents' names and telephone numbers at work; names and telephone numbers of persons to contact in an emergency; name and telephone number of the student's physician; and data from the latest eye report. (A one-page typed list of this information for all your students is a handy reference.)

- *For each school.* Address and telephone number, bell schedule, and map. For each secondary school, also include the master schedule, room-use chart, each student's class schedule with teachers' names and room numbers, and the counselor's name. List the names of additional personnel who work with the students, such as aides, speech and language therapists, occupational therapists, and O&M instructors, and the times they are scheduled to see the students. (You may find it useful to write on one page all your students' schedules and the bell schedules for each school.)

- *Forms.* Lists of materials that have been checked or loaned out, observation forms, and grade forms (see sample forms on pages 48–50).

- *For the district.* The school calendar, directory of schools, map of the school district, mileage chart, mileage and attendance forms (which should be completed each day, since it is easy to forget where you were a few days ago), and schedules for psychologists, nurses, standardized testing, other itinerant teachers, and related services.

MATERIALS

- *Supplies.* Paper (notebook paper, different styles of bold-line paper, typing paper, bold-line graph paper, and braille paper), correction fluid (such as Liquid Paper or Wite-Out), typing correction paper, black felt-tip pens, pencils (Number 2 for test answer sheets and

Materials on Loan

Student _Stephen Young_ Year _90-91_

School _Hillcrest_

Materials Loaned	Location	Date	Return Date	Transferred To	Date
1. Medium reading stand #6	home	9/90			
2. Typing mat #12	home	9/90			
3.					
4. Math in Our World - 6 vols.	Rm. 21	8/90			
5. Macmillan Eng. 3 vols.	"	"			
6. Spelling Wds. + Skills - 1 vol.	"	"			
7. Series R - levels 18, 19, 20, 21, 22,					
8. 23, 24 and worksheets	"	"		Rm. 17	10/90
9. HBJ Science - 2 vols.	"	"			
10. Health + Growth - 1 vol.	"	"			
11. Regions - 2 vols.	"	"	10/90		
12. Medium reading stand #43	"	"			
13. School dist. - 4 vols.	"	10/90			
14. Video magnifier #3 (Aero arm)	"	11/90			
15.					
16. Stopwatch #7	Speech room	3/90			
17. Typing desk	"	12/90			
18. Typing stand #12	"	10/90			
19. Typing mat #7	"	"			
20. You learn to Type - LP - #4	"	"			
21. " " " " - RP - #7	"	"			
22. LP Typewriter # 64248	"	"			
23. Large reading stand #42	"	"			
24.					

Observation Summary

Student __Duane Packard__   Observer __J. Olmstead__

Setting __Classroom / playground__   Date __10/28/90__

Time	Observations	Comments
Classroom 9:00	- Sitting in circle. Raises hand to name a letter at 15'-18'. - Says S for X. [Letter abt. 4" tall]	Check letter recognition.
9:10	- Coloring ditto at 3-4". Difficult staying in line. - Continually stamps feet. - Chin on page - Frequently makes soft sound with lips - Cuts along dotted line with paper at 3". - Aide assists by holding paper as he cuts. - Has trouble following lines.	Coordination problems? Hand motion awkward — assess cutting skills.
Playground 9:30	- Running - Slides down slide 2 times. - Nearly collides with another boy; seems startled. - Bell rings. D. walks to line. - Keeps changing place in line.	1. In circle: move closer to board + teacher + assess vision again. 2. Darken dittos. 3. Verbalize anything demonstrated visually. 4. Extra support from aide good.

49

Grade Summary

Student **Paul Wong** Year **1989-90 / 1990-91**

School **Spenser**

Period	Subject	Teacher	Room	1st Q	2nd Q	1st Sem	3rd Q	4th Q	2nd Sem	Final
1	Eng. 1	Mrs. Doe	213	A[1]	C	B[3,4,6]	D[3]	C[1,3]	D	C
2	Alg. 1	Ms. Smith	225	C	C	C	B	C[3,4]	C	C
3	P.E.	Mr. Jones	gym	D[3,7]	F	F[5]	F[3,4,6]	D[3,6]	D	D
5	Comp. Sci.	Mr. Daniels	336	D[6]	F	F[6,7,9]				
6	Wld. Hist.	Mrs. Peters	114	C[6,7]	D	D[1,6,8]	F[4,6,8,9]	C[2,4,6]	D	D
7	Electronics	Mr. O'Brien	35	C[6]	D	D[2,3,5,7]				
5	Typing	Ms. Lee	242				F[4,6]	C[1,3]	D	D
7	Economics	Mr. Watson	211				D[4]	D[4]	D	D
1	P.E.	Mr. Jones	gym	C[3,7]	D[3,4,7]	D				
2	Eng. 2	Ms. Martin	217	B[4]	C[4,5]	B	B[4,9]	D[2,4,5]	C	C
3	Am. Govt.	Mrs. Brown	26	C	D[3,5]	C	B	C	C	C
5	Typing	Ms. Lee	242	D[2,3]	C	C	C	B	C	C
6	Radio	Mrs. Allen	112	B	A	B	C	B	B	B
7	Alg. 2	Ms. Jenkins	227	D[2,3]	C	D	B	C	C	D
1	Comp. Sci.	Mr. Daniels	336				C	B[1]	B	B

Explanation of Comments

X—Excellent progress
G—Good attitude/conduct
1—Showing some improvement
2—Achievement is not up to apparent ability
3—Absences/tardiness affecting schoolwork
4—Books/materials are not brought to class

5—Assignments are incomplete or unsatisfactory
6—Oral participation needed
7—Inattentive/wastes time/ does not follow directions
8—Conduct in class is not satisfactory
9—(To parents) Please contact teacher through counselor

*Note: The numbers next to some of the grades on this form refer to the Explanation of Commments at the bottom of the form. Readers who adapt this form for their own use may wish to substitute an explanation code from forms used in their districts.

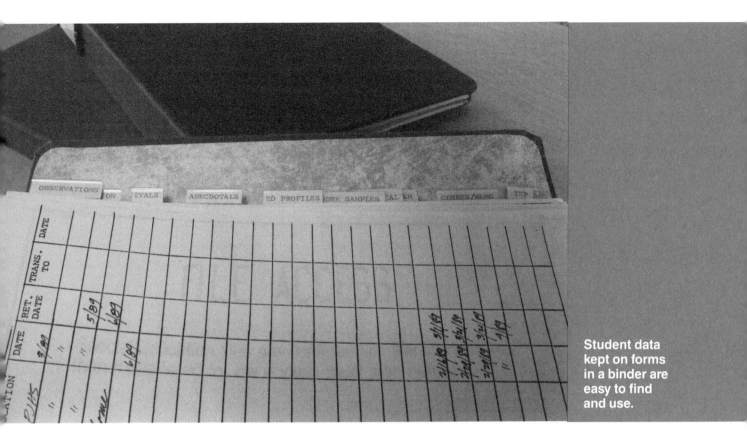

Student data kept on forms in a binder are easy to find and use.

Number 1 for younger children), erasers, a ruler, scissors, chalk, a stapler, self-stick note pads, and a stopwatch. Leave as many of these supplies as possible in a drawer in each of your workrooms so you do not have to carry them from site to site. It is advisable to label the drawers clearly to indicate that the supplies belong to the program for visually impaired students.

■ *Calendar.* Some sort of calendar is essential for keeping track of details on a day-to-day basis. When you get the district calendar, transfer important information to your own calendar so you can see at a glance the dates of special programs or other events that affect scheduling or gathering data. For example, knowing when report cards are distributed lets you check your students' grades at the appropriate times.

■ *Business cards.* Business cards are appropriate to give to eye care specialists, business representatives, and other professionals, as well as to school personnel and families.

■ *Additional forms.* Collect a few copies of every form you may possibly need. Store them in the trunk of your car so they will be available whenever you need them.

Chapter 6 Organization of the Program

IN A DISTRICT WITH several itinerant teachers, a well-organized itinerant program will enhance the effectiveness of each teacher. Basic components include regular staff meetings, appropriate materials, adequate office space and staff, and forms to facilitate organization.

STAFF MEETINGS

Itinerant teachers can be like ships that pass in the night. They often feel isolated from each other. Therefore, in any program with more than one teacher, weekly staff meetings are advisable. These weekly meetings (preferably held at the end of a day) provide teachers with the opportunity to support each other, hear guest speakers, order materials, discuss referrals to the program, plan study trips and in-service programs, and write reports and letters. Regular meetings can generate a more cohesive, effective delivery of services for the students.

MATERIALS

One of the keys to the success of an itinerant program is the availability of an extensive range of supplies, materials, and equipment that are needed to serve a variety of students from ages birth to 21, in regular and special classes, and with mild to severe visual disorders. It can take a long time for a new program to acquire all the supplies in adequate amounts.

Carrying bulky, heavy pieces of equipment from place to place can produce stress, strain, and discomfort. A program should have enough of these items, such as braillers, typewriters, reading-writing stands, and electronic devices, so they can be left at each of the sites where they are used.

It is impossible to list here all the supplies needed by a program, but some of the more crucial items are these:

■ *Computerized equipment.* Computerized devices should be available to students, itinerant teachers, and transcribers to use. The needs of the individuals using the equipment will determine which types should be purchased.

Essential Supplies

- *Electronic magnifying devices.* Having various types of magnifying devices with different options will allow students to use the ones that best enhance their individual visual functioning. The number of devices needed is determined by the visual needs of the students.

- *Electric typewriters.* You should have enough typewriters to be able to leave some in the schools and some in the students' homes when computerized equipment is not available or necessary. You should have some machines with regular-print and some with large-print type.

- *Braillers.* There should be one machine in each classroom where one is needed, one machine in your workroom, and one for the home of each student who uses a brailler.

- *Enlarging copier.* A copier with enlarging capabilities is invaluable for providing materials in the optimum print size for visually impaired students.

- *Audiotape recorders.* Each itinerant teacher should have at least one battery-run, four-track recorder for his or her use. Others should be available for the students' use when necessary.

- *Reading-writing stands.* Having 60 stands for a program that serves 40 students is not excessive. It is not unusual for a student to use 3 stands: 1 in the classroom, 1 in your workroom, and 1 at home. Having different types and sizes lets students experiment to determine which works best for them.

- *Low vision devices.* Accumulate a wide range of monoculars and hand-held and stand magnifiers, some with lights.

- *Lamps.* Having different types of lamps allows students to determine which provides the best illumination for them.

- *Typing stands.* Have one typing stand for each student typist as necessary.

- *Rubber pads.* Use pads under typewriters and braillers to reduce noise and under reading-writing stands to counteract sliding.

- *Typewriter ribbons.* Use heavy- or double-inked ribbons. Discard them when they fade.

- *Stopwatches.* Have at least one for each itinerant teacher to time typing tests and standardized tests.

- *Novels and reference books.* A wide range of books should be purchased in large print or braille, on tape, and, when available, on disk.

- *Paper.* Order a wide range of different types of paper for both braille and print users. If a particular type of bold-line paper is not available, create it yourself and make extras on your copier.

- *Felt-tip pens.* Felt-tip pens can be ordered by the gross to be used by itinerant teachers and distributed to students and their classroom teachers.

- *Correction fluid* (Liquid Paper or Wite-Out, for example). Students who use felt-tip pens can make corrections with correction fluid.

- *Pencils.* Younger elementary school children may choose to use Number 1 pencils with softer lead rather than pens.

In addition, materials should be available pertaining to the development of concepts, vocational skills and awareness, living skills, motor skills, listening skills, academic and visual assessment, academic skills, and visual functioning and disorders. Being aware of and utilizing materials available in the schools reduces the amount you will need to purchase.

Suggested professional reference materials are listed in Appendix D. Sources of catalogs to guide you in ordering supplies and equipment is included in Appendix A.

You may find that you need equipment that is no longer available for purchase or is unavailable in a desired size. District carpenters and shop teachers may be able to make these items for you.

To reduce loss, have people sign out nonconsumable materials carefully. Sign-out cards can be used for items to which an envelope can be attached. The card can stay in the envelope with the item until it is checked out, when the card can be placed in a file behind the borrower's name. Other items, such as typewriters, braillers, and reading-writing stands, can be signed out according to an assigned number; for example, stand Number 34 could be recorded as having gone to a particular school.

OFFICE AND STAFF

A room in a centrally located building in your district is desirable for an office. A telephone, a desk for each teacher, filing cabinets, a copier, a table for meetings, and storage space for materials should be provided.

To expedite locating materials, you can categorize them according to their content and store them according to their categories. It is much easier to find listening-skills materials, for instance, if they are all in one location. A system for classifying materials is presented in Appendix C.

The office may be staffed by a secretary or a transcriber who has the time and is willing to assume additional responsibilities. An efficient, competent worker will take care of many details, freeing the itinerant teacher to spend more time with students. A list of duties includes the following:

■ Preparing materials in braille or large print or on tape or a disk.

■ Maintaining equipment in good repair.

■ Keeping an ongoing tally of federal-quota and district-program budgets and typing orders.

■ Ordering basic supplies as needed.

■ Assisting the itinerant teachers to organize materials in a logical manner.

■ Maintaining a current inventory of materials and equipment.

■ Maintaining a cross-checked system for distributing materials.

■ Answering the telephone.

■ Relaying messages to itinerant teachers in the field.

■ Contacting schools when the itinerant teachers are absent. Pertinent information on an itinerant teacher's absence form (see sample on page 56) enables the secretary to notify the appropriate personnel at each site.

Help from Office Staff

Notification of Itinerant Teacher's Absence

Please fill in the name of the teacher/office to be notified when you are absent.

Teacher _J. Olmstead_   Year _1990-91_

Student	School	Person/Office to Notify
Roger Higgins	Mountain View	Ask secretary to notify teacher (Mr. Smith).
Michael Bell Catherine Aaron Nancy Keller Dan Perry	Park	Ask counselor's clerk at X 3000 to read a note to the students' classes.
Bruce Lowell	Belmont	Ask secretary to tell teacher (Ms. Bennet).
Shirley Chapman	Doyle	Call teacher (Mr. Terry) on classroom phone, X 5000.
Gayle Harper David Moore Ray Jordan	Green Valley	Ask secretary to tell teachers: Ms. Hall, Mr. Wang, Mrs. Collins.

Storing materials by category is an effective way to arrange books and other items.

FORMS

Some forms are helpful for keeping a program of four or five itinerant teachers organized. You can use the samples in Appendix E or create ones that are more useful for your purposes. Using forms standardizes information and makes it easier to find; however, having too many forms can defeat your purpose.

To organize data on students, you may wish to have a binder for each student. Dividers can be used to set up sections for vision reports and data, IEPs, correspondence and memos, observations, anecdotal records, educational profiles, medical information, work samples, and O&M.

Forms are helpful for many reasons. Having information like test results recorded on forms can assist you in analyzing and comparing data (see the sample form on page 58). Also, it can be disheartening to wade through anecdotal records to determine what materials a previous itinerant teacher used with a student. However, the information is readily available if you use a checklist similar to the one presented on pages 59–62. Ongoing data can be recorded on a 5″ × 8″ card for easy reference (see samples on pages 64–65).

When a referral comes to your program from a school served by an itinerant teacher, it is helpful to have that teacher process the referral. Referrals from other schools can be assigned to teachers on a rotating basis. It is a good idea to keep a record of referrals to the program (see sample form on page 63).

If a referral is "closed" or not accepted to the program, keep the information you collected in the back of a file cabinet. Students are often rereferred, so it is helpful to have records of your initial screenings.

Academic Tests Summary

Student _Marian Brown_   Date of Birth _6/10/81_

Test _California Achievement Test_   Date _5/14/88_
            (CAT)

Scores: Reading 33/4
         Vocabulary 43/5
         Math 65/6

Comments:

scores: percentage/stanine

- LP copy
- time and a half - didn't need it
- marked answers on test booklet
- aide marked answer sheet

Test _CAT_   Date _5/22/89_

Scores: Reading 60/6   %/stanine
         Vocabulary 50/5
         Math 51/5

Comments:

- same as above
- resisted using LP copy

Test _CAT_   Date _5/18/90_
       %/stanine

Scores: Reading 58/5
         Vocabulary 47/5
Comments: Math 26/4
         Spelling 70/6

- Conditions same as 5/88
- needed extra time for math

- check re: extra help for math

Student Checklist

M: Mastered area/skill
C: Continue instruction or use
E: Exposed to area/skill

Name ___TOM CAITLEN___

Teacher's Initials	N.K.	N.K.	J.O.
School Year	19 87 to 19 88	19 88 to 19 89	19 89 to 19 90
Information about Visual Impairment			
Myopia, nystagmus	E, C	E, C	C, C
Visual acuity and significance		E, C	C, C
model of eye		E, C	C, C
Vision Assessments			
Near vision	✓	✓	✓
Intermediate vision	✓		✓
Stereopsis/binocularity	✓		✓
Color	✓		
Tracking	✓	✓	
Cover/uncover	✓		✓
Reading speed- regular print			✓
Reading speed- large print			✓
Distance vision			✓
Optical Aids			
Amber slip-ins	E	E	
Reading stand (small/large) and pad	M, C	M, C	M, C
No.1 pencils, felt-tip pens, bold-line paper	C	C	C
	M, C	M, C	M, C
Amber filter for dittos		E	C
Sunshade			C

Note: The categories and key used in this form can be adapted or changed for the reader's use.

Teacher's Initials	N.K.	N.K.	J.O.
School Year	19 87 to 19 88	19 88 to 19 89	19 89 to 19 90
Instructional Materials			
Reading			
Mathematics			
Fingermath	C	C	C
Telling time	C	C	
Addition, subtraction flashcards	C	M	
+, - Quizmo	C	M	
Moving Up in Time			C
Teacher's Initials	N.K.	N.K.	J.O.
School Year	19 87 to 19 88	19 88 to 19 89	19 89 to 19 90

Teacher's Initials	N.K.	N.K.	J.B.
School Year	19 87 to 19 88	19 88 to 19 89	19 89 to 19 90
Language/Spelling			
Moving up in Grammar:		C	C
Capitalization + Punctuation			
Alphabetizing exercises		C	C
Punctuation exercises			C
Handwriting			
Peter Possum upper-and lower-case manuscript	C	M	
New Links to Cursive			C knows all lower-case + b, g, m, n
Typing Manual			
You Learn to Type			to p. 34
Computers			
Apple in class	✓	✓	
Apple in lab			✓

Teacher's Initials	N.K.	N.K.	J.O.
School Year	19 87 to 19 88	19 88 to 19 89	19 89 to 19 90
Career Education			
Summer school	E	E	C
Living Skills			
Department store math	E,C	E,C	m
Money Bingo	E,C	E,C	m
Money Dominoes		E,C	m
Judy Clock		E,C	C,C
Auditory Skills			
Library books	C		
Listen + Learn		C	C
Simon			C
Games			
Hangman- spelling words	C	C	C
Miscellaneous			
Cal. achievement - marked answers test enlarged 154% on copy	C	C	C
Copying from chalkboard		C	C

Program Referrals

Date	Name	Referred By	Investigating Teacher	School	Date of IEP or Closing	Date of Closing	Reason for Closing
10/89	Sally Doe	School Study Team	Mary Jenning	Jenning	5/4/90		
11/89	Ellen Jones	"	Barbara	Green		4/5/90	DNQ (didn't qualify)
11/89	Peter Smith	"	Ron	Central	1/11/90		
12/89	John Martin	Mr. Freene	Barbara	Jenning			
1/22/90	Sean O'Grady	Mr. Jones	Mary	Sunset		2/15/90	DNQ
2/25/90	Helen Brown	Mrs. Wing	Barbara	Weller		3/24/90	moved out of district
3/2/90	Joseph Denis	Paul King	Ron	Summit	3/9/90		
3/12/90	Nick Pullman	Parents	Mary	Triddle			

Student Data Card

Name _Ray Johnson_ Parent(s) Name _Helen + Roscoe Johnson_

Date of Birth _1/1/73_ Address _10 Main Street, Westview 00003_ Student I.D. # _00033_

Home Phone _321-4567_ Emergency Phone _777-1122_ Work Phone Mother _765-4321_ Father _234-2340_

Year	Itinerant Teacher	School of Attendance	School in Resident District	Gr.	Special Class	Reading Level	BL PS Print Used	Bus	Other
1980-81	Jackson	Dickson	Jennings	2	yes	1	BL LP yes	yes	
1981-82	O'Neill	"	"	3	"	"	" " "	"	
1982-83	Watson	"	"	4	"	3.2	" " "	"	
1983-84	Gonzalez	"	"	5	"	4	" " "	"	
1984-85	Jones	"	"	6	"	5	" " "	"	
1985-86	Smith	Central	Central	7	no	6	PS no no	"	
1986-87	Olmstead	"	"	8	"		" " "	"	
1987-88	Doe	Fredericks	Wicks	9	"		" " "	"	
1988-89	Davis	"	"	10	"		" " "	"	
1989-90	Waters	Spenser	"	11	"		" " "	"	
1990-91	Olmstead	"	"	12	"		" " "	"	

Gr. = Grade   BL = Legally Blind   PS = Partially Sighted

Student Data Card (side 2)

RFB # __222222__ LOC __10/84__ Rehab. __6/90__ Transit I.D. __No__ SS # __333-33-3333__

Hospital _____ Doctor _____ Medical # _____

Eye Condition __Albinism, nystagmus__ Entered Program __10/80__

Vision Reports __11/84, 2/85, 12/87__ Low Vision Exam __2/85 Dr. Smith__

O&M Received __1982-83__
__1985-86__
__1987-88__

Other Handicaps __None__

Acuity: __10/80 ; 10/80 w/cor.__
__R- 20/200 ; L 20/70__

Comments __Prim Hand Code 31-VI__
__monocular prescribed + purchased__
__3/85__

Psychological Evaluation __1988__

Passed Proficiency __X__

Graduated __6/90__

or Left Program _____

RFB = Recording for the Blind   LOC = Library of Congress   Rehab. = Department of Rehabilitation   SS = Social Security   O&M = Orientation & Mobility

65

Chapter 7

Relationships and Responsibilities in Schools

YOUR STUDENTS' progress and participation in school activities can be enhanced by your relationship with the faculty and staff. The better the rapport, the more the school staff will support and cooperate with you to provide an effective program for the visually impaired students.

BE VISIBLE

At the start of the year, make an appointment with the appropriate administrator in each school to discuss the needs of the visually impaired students, your role, and whatever special arrangements you need (such as a workroom, mailbox, and provisions for using the school copier). Make sure you are introduced to the teachers and support staff (secretaries, clerks, custodians, counselors, nurses, and so on), and maintain good relationships with them; they can provide crucial information and support.

Give copies of your schedule (see the sample schedule on page 68) at each school to appropriate personnel (administrators, secretaries, counselors, the students' teachers, the nurse, the psychologist, and so forth). If you write the schedule on a small piece of paper, secretaries with glass on their desks can slip it under the glass.

The first faculty meeting of the year is usually when new teachers are introduced. You may wish to be introduced then, too.

ADAPT

Evaluate and fit into the atmosphere of each school; each is different. Some schools are more structured than are others. In some schools, you may need to go through a lengthy process to do something special; others may have a more laissez-faire attitude. The more you fit in, the more you will be accepted.

Classroom teachers often have their own special chairs in faculty rooms. Wise itinerant teachers make sure they are not offending these teachers by sitting in their favorite chairs.

Sometimes you may find it difficult to get a problem solved at a school. A friendly, reliable teacher in the faculty room may be willing to share some insights about how to resolve a difficulty at that particular site.

1988-89 Schedule—Grant

Jean Olmstead
Teacher of the Visually Impaired
Office phone: 320-4500

Day	Student	Time	Room
Mondays	Donna Chapman	10:10-10:40	Classroom or Library
Tuesdays	Donna Chapman	8:30-9:00	Speech/Vision Room
	Joan Freeman	9:00-9:30	
	William Watkins	9:40-10:10	
	Gregory Sherman	10:10-10:40	
Thursdays	Donna Chapman	8:30-9:00	Speech/Vision Room
	Joan Freeman	9:00-9:30	
Fridays	William Watkins	8:30-9:15	Speech/Vision Room
	Gregory Sherman	9:40-10:25	

BE SENSITIVE AND REALISTIC

Realistically, in an itinerant program all dittos cannot be transcribed and all learning situations cannot be ideal for the visually impaired students. Your students are mainstreamed because they can adjust and adapt to such situations and be responsible for requesting assistance when they need it.

Keep in mind all the demands placed on classroom teachers. Whenever a traveling teacher comes to a school, there is more work for the administrators, faculty members, and staff. Be gracious in acknowledging their extra efforts. Repay them with favors when possible. Treats for the faculty room will be appreciated.

If it is permitted in your district, one way to help the classroom teacher is to use reverse mainstreaming by including some of his or her students when you work with the visually impaired student. For example, if the visually impaired student needs to work on making change, you may choose to have him or her play an appropriate game with some classmates who need help with that skill. Doing so will not only help the classroom teacher but may benefit the visually impaired student academically and socially.

Finally, follow the rules. In a hurried day of traveling from school to school, it is sometimes tempting to circumvent some rules, such as signing in when you arrive and signing out when you leave. Allow adequate time to follow the procedures of your district and those of each school.

Chapter 8

Your Rights in Schools

A S YOU HAVE responsibilities in schools, such as following rules and procedures, so should the district have responsibilities regarding your working conditions. Administrators have an obligation to provide you with the basic accommodations that other teachers receive: an appropriate room, furniture suited to instructional needs, keys, a mailbox, and a safe place to store equipment. Your time at each site is limited; having to move equipment around and look for a workroom on a frequent basis robs you and your student of valuable time together. If necessary, the basic accommodations and rights outlined here should be bargained for in the contract between the school district and the teachers' representatives.

AN APPROPRIATE ROOM

Good lighting, privacy, consistent accessibility, space for necessary furniture, and a place to store materials and equipment safely are requisites for a room, as are heat and windows. Establishing your schedule relatively early in the year may ensure that you have an adequate work space in each school.

Sometimes you may try two or three rooms before you find an appropriate one. Often you will use a room that someone else uses at other times. Be diplomatic and tactful yet aggressive in your efforts to obtain a suitable space in which to work.

Other itinerant or on-site personnel may use your assigned rooms for various purposes. Some schools may post room-use schedules. If not, you may tape to the door a form like the one presented on page 70 to reduce conflicts.

KEYS AND MAILBOX

Needed keys should be easily accessible or lent to you for the school year. If you have several school keys, you may choose to put them on a separate key ring from your car keys and take them into schools only when you need them.

Having a mailbox at each school served is essential. To communicate with other teachers, you must have a mailbox. Because your time is limited at each school, much contact with classroom teachers is carried out via notes regarding materials to be transcribed, class activities, and your students' participation.

To all personnel: Please indicate the day and time you regularly use this room.

Year ___1989-90___

Time	Monday	Tuesday	Wednesday	Thursday	Friday
8:00					
9:00					
10:00					
11:00	G. Olmstead Vision Specialist		G. Olmstead Vision Specialist		
12:00					G. Olmstead Vision Specialist
1:00					
2:00					
3:00					

A mailbox is also helpful for finding out what is going on in each school. Ask the secretary to put *all* notices for school personnel in your box. You will then receive some extraneous handouts but will also learn about field trips, special schedules, testing, school activities, or special programs that may affect or interest your student.

SAFE, SECURE STORAGE

Leave necessary equipment at each school. Carrying a large-print typewriter to three or four schools per day quickly diminishes the joy of itinerant teaching. Ideally, the equipment is stored in the room that only you use. Realistically, the room is used by more than one person, or equipment must be stored in another location. If the equipment is at another location, make sure it is close enough to your room so you can carry it easily. When your materials are in rooms used by other personnel, be sure to label them clearly, as in the following example:

Table for Visually Impaired Program
Please do not remove during school year 1990-1991

Jean Olmstead
Itinerant Teacher, Visually Impaired
320-4500

PREPARATION AND LUNCHTIME

Travel time between schools does not constitute preparation time. Conference-preparation periods should be available to you just as they are to other teachers so you can make and receive telephone calls, write reports, and prepare for lessons with students.

A spacious, well-organized workroom.

Less-than-ideal working conditions.

Each teacher should be guaranteed the standard district-approved lunch period in addition to travel time; eating while driving does not lend itself to safe driving practices or a healthy state of mind or body. You should have the right to schedule a lunch period for yourself at an appropriate time each day, even though you may find yourself typing a last-minute ditto or proofreading during that time.

USE OF DISTRICT CARS

Some itinerant teachers believe that because districts provide major pieces of equipment for classroom teachers to fulfill their roles, district cars should be provided for itinerant teachers, since itinerant teachers need them to fulfill their duties. If a district car is not available for your use, reimbursement for mileage should be adequate to cover the costs of using your personal vehicle (gasoline, repairs, insurance, depreciation, and so on).

Chapter 9

Other Essentials

ITINERANT TEACHERS deal with a number of concerns and issues that regular classroom teachers do not. Many of these issues relate to the fact that traveling instead of being continuously present at one site is in the nature of the job.

ABSENCES

Of Students

One of the most frustrating experiences an itinerant teacher will encounter is to dash madly into a school and breathlessly set up equipment only to discover that the visually impaired student is absent. Inform parents of your schedule (see sample forms on page 74), and ask them to call you or your office when their child is absent on your scheduled day. Some students, from ages 10 to 12 on, can be expected to call you themselves; teach them to use the telephone, and encourage them to take this responsibility. You may ask school personnel (a secretary, a teacher, or an attendance clerk) to call you when your student is absent, but notification by the student or parent is usually more reliable.

Of Teachers

Itinerant teachers usually have substitutes only for long-term absences. When you schedule a student, inform the appropriate teacher that when you are absent, the student will come to or remain in class. In some instances (usually in elementary schools), the student waits for you to get him or her from class; all you have to do is let the teacher know, via the secretary, that you will not be there that day.

In secondary schools, in which the student comes to you for a full period, an appropriate staff member can notify the student of your absence by sending a note to him or her during the first-period class. If you are to see a secondary school student during the first period, call the student at home early in the morning to tell him or her to go to the regular first-period class.

You may work with some secondary school students for a full period at the same time every day. At the beginning of the school year, you should arrange for a place such as the library where these students can spend the period when you are absent.

To: *Janice Rivera*

Year: *1990-91*

I have listed below the days and times I will be working with you this year. Please call my office to let me know when you are absent on one of those days.

Mondays : 8:30 - 9:00

Wednesdays : 11:10 - 11:40

Thursdays : 8:30 - 9:00

Thank you,

Mrs. Olmstead

Mrs. Olmstead
320-4500

Dear Mrs. Olmstead,

I have read your schedule of days and times to work with *Janice*. I will help *Janice* remember to call you if he/she is absent on a day when you come to work with him/her.

Rosa Rivera
Parent's Signature

9/24/89
Date

Sometimes special events necessitate a change in schedule. Notify the principal and teacher involved before your absence with a form similar to the one on page 75.

When a classroom teacher is absent, the substitute would be more effective if he or she had some information about the visually impaired student's participation in activities. The form presented on page 76 is set up to be signed by the classroom teacher and left with the lesson plans.

To: _____Mr. Smith_____

Date: _____5/25/90_____

Because of a scheduling conflict, I will be unable to be at your school at the following time(s):

10:00 – Thursday, May 28
Ellen Newhall will come to P.E.

_____Jean Olmstead_____
Jean Olmstead
Itinerant Teacher, Visually Impaired
320-4500

ADDITIONAL STRATEGIC POINTS

Extended Year (Summer School)

A summer school class for visually impaired students has several important benefits. The students can work on skills, such as motor development, cooking, and cleaning, that are sometimes difficult to teach on an itinerant basis during the school year. They can also participate in group discussions regarding visual impairments and remediation devices and techniques.

You may be involved in recommending that a summer school class be established and in suggesting which students on your caseload would benefit from attending the class. It is helpful to prepare for the teacher of the class a list of skills on which each student should concentrate.

Students' Lockers

By keeping a record of students' locker combinations, you can help students if they have problems opening their lockers. Special click or magnetic locks are available for those who have difficulty opening the regular locks.

Many schools are reducing hallway lighting to conserve electricity, which makes it more difficult for some visually impaired students to see the numbers on their locks. A staff member on site can change a student's locker to one in a more well-lit area or even to one closer to eye level. Using penlights for extra lighting when they open their lockers may help some students open them more easily.

Date: 10/5/90

To My Substitute:

Please be aware that _Steve Young_ is in my _4th_ period
class. _Steve_ is a visually impaired student and reads
in braille.

Please remember that

1. Anything you write on the board will need to be verbalized and,

2. During fire drills or disaster drills, you will need to take extra care to make sure this student is safe. I have made the following special arrangements to ensure his/her safety:

Fire drills/evacuations: Tom Jordan, Phil Cross, or Janice Partner will assist Steve.

3. Other: _Steve's handouts are with the other students. If Steve needs extra assistance, he will let you know. He is a capable student._

Should you have other questions or concerns, talk with _Mr. Johnson, our Counselor_ here at the school, or contact
the teacher of the visually impaired, _Jean Olmstead_
at _320-4500_.

Sincerely,

Janet Grimes

A student using a penlight while opening a locker.

Location of Offices and Teachers

Finding the main office at a new school may be confusing if the building has several doors or there are several buildings in the complex. The door or building closest to the school's flagpole is usually close to the main office. If you are looking for a staff person who is not in his or her assigned location, check with the main office for the person's whereabouts. Some schools post pictures of faculty and staff members or have yearbooks available in the faculty room or office. To identify a staff member for the first time, you may ask to see a picture of him or her.

Food and Weather

Eating cottage cheese that is 110 degrees from being in a hot car all morning is unhealthy. Insulated bags with ice packs are readily available and are a wonderful boon for the traveling teacher. It will be easier to carry the lunch bag into a school with the rest of your materials if the bag has a shoulder strap.

In rainy weather, a poncho may be sufficient protection. It generally covers all the paraphernalia toted around and, unlike an umbrella, does not add to the number of items to be carried.

YOUR CAR AND RELATED ISSUES

If you have a choice of vehicles, the most helpful kind has four doors and safe storage in the trunk or under the hatchback. Be prepared to carry a lot of materials and papers in your car. Organizing your gear will reduce your frustrations. Cloth totebags and plastic crates or containers are useful for organizing materials you cannot leave on site.

Logistics

Keep software in a cooler or other insulated container so it will not overheat in hot weather, and carry it in plastic bags or holders in case of rain. In hot weather, a shield for the front windshield may reduce the buildup of heat. Also available is a solar car ventilator that keeps the interior temperature the same as the exterior by recycling the inside air periodically.

If your car can be locked without using a key, you may choose to carry a spare key with

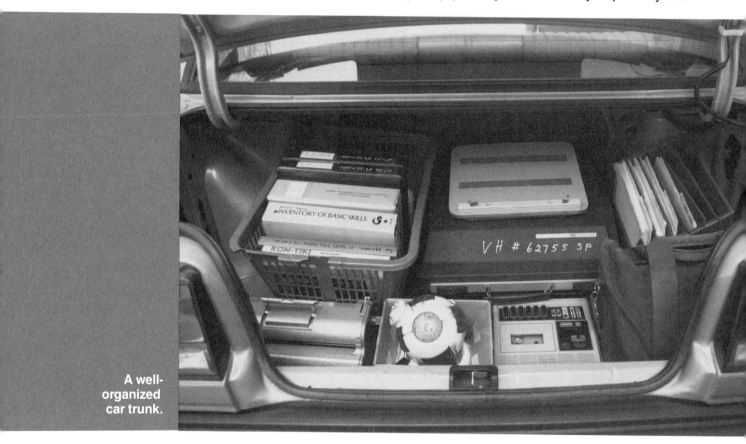

A well-organized car trunk.

you or have one in a magnetic container hidden under your car in case you inadvertently lock your keys in your car.

On dark, rainy, or foggy days you may drive with your headlights on for safety reasons. Develop a strategy for ensuring that your headlights are off when you park. For example, you can make it a habit to check your headlight switch every time you remove your keys from the ignition.

If your mileage reimbursement for any given year is less than the standard rate allowed by the federal government, you may deduct a percentage of your automobile expenses and depreciation on your income tax return. To do so, keep good records of your car-related expenditures, total mileage, and mileage used for professional purposes.

Parking and Commuting

Parking at some schools, particularly secondary schools, can be difficult. Some schools may assign a numbered space to you; others may require a sticker to park in the faculty lot. You may request a special parking space close to the entrance because of the heavy materials you unload and the time constraints inherent in being itinerant.

Overall, itinerant teachers often spend a good part of their workdays in their cars. You may find it advisable if you can to live close to the school district or area in which you teach to minimize the amount of time you spend driving.

FINAL WORDS OF WISDOM

I hope you find the suggestions and information in this book helpful. I have provided a lot of information, but I certainly have not answered all the questions that arise for itinerant teachers. In fact, for some questions, there are no absolute answers.

The strategies I have outlined are not the only ones to use. Many fine itinerant teachers do things differently, and their procedures are just as correct as the ones presented here. One wish I had as I wrote this book is that a dialogue among itinerant teachers will grow and that we will meet more often at conferences and in small groups and be more willing to share our ideas in publications and newsletters. Because we are relatively isolated from our peers, we often feel that the itinerant teacher in the next county has the answers to the concerns that confound us. The truth is that each experienced teacher has some good strategies to share and some issues for which he or she is searching for solutions.

Another wish is that working conditions will improve for itinerant teachers as others realize the complexities of our role and recognize that many of the students served in itinerant programs require more extensive intervention than they are receiving. Overloading teachers with too many students at too many sites robs the students of the important assistance they need to attain competencies in critical areas.

I have offered suggestions for organizational structures, but flexibility is a key trait of any successful itinerant teacher. There are too many situations that we cannot control, and we need to be able to change at any given moment as conditions demand change. Murphy's law states that if anything can go wrong, it will. As we deal with the challenges and demands of our jobs, it may sometimes seem as though Murphy was an optimist. My best suggestion is to avoid letting the changing conditions affect us adversely, meet them with equanimity and a sense of humor, strive for a realistic perspective of what is important, and keep them from detracting from the services we provide to visually impaired students and from our sense of satisfaction in doing so.

A Rural Perspective

By Jane Stewart

RURAL ITINERANT PROGRAMS for visually impaired students are similar to urban and suburban programs, except for the many miles traveled between schools and the kinds of program options available. Although state regulations require a full range of program options for visually impaired children, usually the only real options for visually impaired children in rural areas are the state school and the itinerant program. The rural itinerant teacher often must drive hundreds of miles to see one student, then turn around and drive back, wondering, "What did I 'do' today?"

But rural programs can be great for many reasons. First, rural people care about "their own." The communities are generally close knit. When approached tactfully, schools, workplaces, and churches and other religious institutions are glad to help further the skills of a disabled child. The schools are a major source of pride for the communities. Frequently, they are the major meeting places in the community for adults and for after-school activities for children. Establishing good relationships with the principal and key teachers will truly help further the skills of your student.

Second, rural people care about you—the itinerant teacher. The classroom teachers and parents are thrilled to see that someone knows how to help educate a visually impaired child, so the child can continue living at home. They can be there to help you in many ways. One itinerant teacher convinced a local bridge club to hand enlarge textbooks for a certain visually impaired student. The women put their cards away and met all summer long to complete those textbooks—and not one of them was related to the student! Later, the same teacher taught several of the women to braille. She now has a great source of volunteer braillists for her students.

The information in this book is important to the rural itinerant teacher. You, like your counterpart in the city, will have to adhere to the regulations of the Education for All Handicapped Children Act (P.L. 94–142), develop IEPs, write lesson plans, keep progress notes, order materials, and so on. But here are a few specific ideas to help you—the rural itinerant teacher.

DEALING WITH ALONENESS

Your Isolation

When you are an itinerant teacher in a rural area, you are usually the only teacher of visually impaired students for miles—probably counties. You are expected to know everything about visually impaired children, from the gifted ones to the severely or profoundly retarded ones, and from braille readers to readers of regular print. There is often no one for you to talk with about the problems you encounter. What do you do?

You will find it helpful to keep in touch with other teachers of visually impaired children. Become pen pals with neighboring itinerant teachers. Start an informal newsletter with them. Just jot down ideas and notes—nothing formal, or you will find it becomes a chore—and start an ongoing letter. If you are a first-year teacher, keep in touch with the other teachers with whom you graduated; you will generally feel more comfortable with them than you will with the neighboring teachers of visually impaired students who are strangers to you. Whomever you write to, however, remember to keep your students' names and other identifying information confidential.

Join professional organizations. Attend state and regional conferences annually. Most administrators and supervisors of itinerant programs understand the issue of professional "aloneness" and are willing to let you attend conferences, and some require you to attend them.

Finally, expand your concept of teaching visually impaired children. Learn from teachers in other disciplines, such as those who teach hearing impaired, multidisabled, and learning disabled students. You will learn a lot, and learning from other teachers is a good way to teach them about visually impaired children.

Isolation of Students and Parents

The feelings of aloneness experienced by visually impaired children and their parents also need to be dealt with and frequently are more difficult to handle than your own. Administrators may often understand the need for the teacher to have contact with other teachers but may not recognize the need for the student to be with other students or the parents to be with other parents. So try the newsletter again. This time, have the students and parents write it, and you coordinate it. Incorporate newsletter articles into IEP objectives for typing, handwriting, and so on. The articles can be about things that a typical child (who happens to be visually impaired) may do, as well as awards received, other honors, and interesting events. Parents can write similar articles about their activities, and questions and answers about resources, self-help concerns, support groups, and the like can also be included.

In addition, try to arrange for pen pals among your students and act as "mail clerk" for the pen pals you have set up. Children enjoy receiving letters from other students. You can match up students with similar interests and those who help each other with skills, such as by pairing a student with good braille skills with a student who has poorer braille skills.

Also try "exchange days." Have one visually impaired student visit another visually impaired student's school for a day or part of a day. It is a great learning experience for the student and can be an even better experience for the student's sighted classmates. Have exchange days with pen pals as well.

USING 'WINDSHIELD' TIME

Driving can be a good time to think through lesson plans, IEP objectives, presentations for parents' groups, conversations with parents, and so on, provided that you can also keep your mind on the road. Keep a tape recorder in your car for your use (a voice-activated one is great). Then record notes on the recorder while you are driving. You can also review the students' tapes. But do not try to write out notes or lessons while driving. You are asking for an accident. Some people eat their lunch in the car, then use their lunchtime to take a walk to restore their energy. This can be hazardous, though, so if you are inclined to eat while driving, do not become overly involved with the food instead of the road.

Finally, remember that driving is meant to get you from one place to another. A lot of driving is expected in your job. If you cannot safely drive and record, listen, or eat at the same time, do not do so. Relax and just drive.

GETTING GOOD DIRECTIONS

For a person who has never lived in a rural environment, interpreting directions may be the biggest challenge. To a "city" person, some of the vocabulary rural people use may sound foreign. Terms like "the four lane," "the blacktop," "the old man's farmhouse," "a-ways," and "a piece" are common. It took me a while before I understood that "the four lane" was the interstate highway, "the blacktop" was any "out of town" asphalt road, and the "old man's farmhouse" was a field where a farmhouse used to stand—20 years ago. "A-ways" and "a piece" seem to be definitely defined terms, but I have not really figured them out yet. I have learned through experience that "a-ways" is a lesser distance then "a piece."

Another trick is to figure out how blacktops are named. When I was new to rural areas, I had difficulty figuring out how one road had two names. For example, if I were talking to a man from Joppa, the road would be called the Metropolis road. If I were talking to a man from Metropolis, the same road would be called the Joppa road. I soon realized that the road's name is determined by the name of the town to which you are heading.

Directions obtained from a local person may be filled with landmarks that relate to an event that occurred long ago or bear the name of a person who is dead. "Turn left at the Johnsons' farm" sounds harmless, but the Johnsons may have been the original owners and the Smiths now have their name on the mailbox. You could be lost for days! So get specific information about the distance to be traveled; the position, color, and size of the landmark; and so forth. Rural people also like to use compass directions. Therefore, put a compass in your car.

The best way to get good, useful directions is to call your destination—the school, home, or business—before you leave your office. Or ask someone in your office how to get there.

MAINTAINING YOUR CAR

Your car is your office, your faculty room, and your best friend. In many rural itinerant programs, you will be in your car more than half your workday. Your car needs special care to keep you happy.

Choose a car that you will be comfortable in, one that gets excellent gas mileage, and one you like. Keep it in good repair. Take care of your scheduled maintenance checks. Check the

**Classic
itinerant pose.**

oil regularly. If you do not know much about cars, find a friendly mechanic to teach you the basics. Remember to learn to change a tire.

You may consider joining an organization like the American Automobile Association. But before you do, make sure its services extend to your area.

Finally, and most important, as a rural driver, carry some special equipment in your car in case of an emergency. These items might include a gallon of water (for you and for the car), blankets, a small shovel, flares, high-energy snacks, and the most frequently used items—a pair of casual slacks and sneakers. The last two items are for those days when you are all dressed up and you get a flat tire.

DEALING WITH ABSENCES AND UNSCHEDULED SCHOOL CLOSINGS

The most frustrating experience in a rural program is to drive for hours only to discover that your student is absent. The best way to avoid this situation is to let everyone—from the classroom teacher, principal, secretaries, and janitors to parents and students—know your schedule and the telephone numbers where you can be reached throughout the day. Give each of these persons copies of your weekly schedule, which should include the time, school, town, telephone number, and contact person for each of the places where you will be, so there is no question about where they can call in case of an absence. In bold print at the top of this schedule put your name, position, and office telephone number. If your office has a toll-free

ITINERANT TEACHING

number, post it on the top of your schedule. When a person has remembered to call you about a student's absence, send a thank-you note to show your appreciation.

Some parents will always let you know when their children will be out of school. Give some of them your home telephone number so they can call you early in the morning if their child is going to be absent. (Be cautious about giving your number out—this information can be abused.)

I have had one chronically absent student. After I made several useless trips to the school, the parent and I made an agreement that I would call their home at 7:00 A.M. on the days I was to see the student, just to make sure she would be in school. In one year, this process saved me seven trips to a school that is three hours from my office; it has cost my district about $5.00 in telephone calls from my home phone (I am reimbursed) and has saved the district over $500 in useless travel money.

I have also invited parents or responsible students to call my home or my office collect in case of absence or snow days. Letting them call me collect means that the district assumes the expense of the call.

If you are not informed when a student is absent, you can still use your time at the school wisely. You can use that time to meet with teachers or other school staff, observe your student's classroom, check out classrooms and teachers for next year, check out areas for mobility lessons, tackle some of the stacks of paperwork you have been putting off, or read professional materials that you keep in your car for instances just like this.

It can be difficult for a teacher who travels through many counties to keep up with unscheduled school closings for snow and other types of poor weather, heating or cooling problems, and so on. The weather may be clear in your area and terrible just a few miles away; although your office may not be closed, one of your schools may be. Therefore, close contact with the school principals is important. Many schools have developed "phone chains" to inform personnel of closings. Become part of that chain in every school where you have a student.

Another problem arises when you get stuck at a school because of bad weather and cannot get to your home that evening. Be prepared in advance. Check your employer's policy on reimbursing you for staying at hotels or motels in such cases. Many rural communities do not have hotels (at least ones you would want to stay overnight in), so you may want to become "buddies" with someone in the area—in case you need to spend the night. Always carry a few emergency items in case you get stranded—a change of warm clothing, a toothbrush, necessary medications, and so on.

CONSIDERING PROGRAM OPTIONS

As stated earlier in this chapter, in rural areas, there are generally only two program options for educating a visually impaired child—an itinerant program and a state school. When determining a student's placement, it is essential to consider the student's needs. Itinerant programs do not meet the needs of all visually impaired students, and alternatives must be weighed.

Perhaps your program and the program from a neighboring area could jointly open a resource room between your two areas. Or perhaps you could arrange an "open door" policy with the state school so a student could attend the school for a specified amount of time to learn specific skills.

All itinerant teachers (including teachers of visually impaired children) must be realistic about what they can accomplish in an itinerant program. Furthermore, teachers in rural itinerant programs need to use a team approach and communicate frequently with all the people who work with a student. When you are with a student only for a limited amount of time, other team members must know about and be able to reinforce the skills you are teaching.

WORKING WITH ASSISTANTS AND PARAPROFESSIONALS

You may find a greater use of teacher assistants or paraprofessionals in rural programs for visually impaired children. Depending on how your area is funded, these assistants may be hired through your office or through the districts in which the students attend school. These assistants may be stationary (that is, assigned to one student at one school) or itinerant.

The primary job of an assistant is usually to prepare materials when you are not there, not to instruct the students. In general, teacher assistants who work with visually impaired children will need to be trained to read and to write braille, to prepare large-print materials, or to prepare both braille and large-print materials. It is usually the itinerant teacher's responsibility to provide the training. Although on-the-job training can be effective, it may be more efficient to meet with the teacher assistants at a special time during the week, once or twice a week for an hour or more, until training is completed. (Training in how to prepare large-print materials will be considerably shorter than training related to braille.) Include information about other compensatory skills during the training so that the assistants are aware of the scope of the students' needs. Skills training can be done through a correspondence course as well as at a central location.

The responsibilities of teacher assistants vary from one district to another. To have knowledgeable assistants, you can arrange for a one-day in-service meeting annually that the assistants must attend, in which you discuss program concerns and individual problems and their solutions, as well as responsibilities and differences in the curricula of the various districts. Speakers and workshops can address topics that are pertinent to the current needs of the assistants.

Assistants can be among the best assets of an itinerant teacher. They are generally persons from the local area who have wide contacts. Treat them as the professionals they are.

WHO'S MY BOSS?

Many rural itinerant programs are regionally based, containing several special education cooperatives or districts. Within this structure, you may have many "bosses." This situation can be confusing for itinerant teachers. You may be dealing with one director of special education at a regional level and another at the district level. You may work with a vision supervisor, a state supervisor, and principals of schools who all think that you are "theirs"! Therefore, deal with each person in the best way you see fit, but also remember who is employing you.

Appendix A

Sources of Materials and Equipment

Providing materials for meeting the individual needs of your students is an important aspect of your role. You will find it helpful to be on many mailing lists to receive catalogs and information about products. The following is a list of companies and organizations from which you may obtain equipment and materials; brief descriptions of the products available are included. Order materials as you need them, but do not wait until your supplies are depleted. Delivery of products may not occur until two months after you send in a purchase requisition.

American Foundation for the Blind
15 West 16th Street
New York, NY 10011
(212) 620-2000 or (800) 232-5463
A great variety of books and pamphlets on topics relating to blindness and visual impairment; a great range of products for independent living for blind and visually impaired people, including games, measuring devices, and educational aids.

American Optometric Association
243 North Lindbergh Boulevard
St. Louis, MO 63141
(314) 991-4100
Pamphlets about vision and visual impairments; models of the eye.

American Printing House for the Blind
P.O. Box 6085
Louisville, KY 40206
(502) 895-2405
A wide variety of books in braille and large print; educational materials and equipment for visually impaired students, including speech synthesizers and other computer equipment, educational software, and braille computer paper.

American Thermoform Corporation
2311 Travers Avenue
City of Commerce, CA 90040
(213) 723-9021
Materials and equipment for reproducing materials in braille, including embossers, computer paper, and other related equipment.

Beckley-Cardy Corporation
1 East First Street
Duluth, MN 55802
(800) 227-1178

A wide selection of office and educational supplies and materials.

Bernell Corporation
P.O. Box 4637
South Bend, IN 46634
(213) 234-3200 or (800) 348-2225

Vision assessment supplies; magnification aids and other optical low vision devices.

Exceptional Teaching Aids
20102 Woodbine Avenue
Castro Valley, CA 94546
(415) 582-4859

Educational materials and equipment for visually impaired students, including tutorial and other educational software; braille materials for reading readiness, math readiness, and math practice; and books on cassette.

Howe Press
Perkins School for the Blind
175 North Beacon Street
Watertown, MA 02172
(617) 924-3490

Materials and equipment for reproducing materials in braille, including Perkins Braillers and accessories, brailling slates and accessories, handwriting and mathematical aids, braille paper, measuring devices, games, and drawing supplies.

Independent Living Aids
27 East Mall
Plainview, NY 11803
(516) 752-8080 or (800) 537-2118

A wide variety of devices for people who are visually impaired, hearing impaired, or physically impaired, including braille slates and writing aids, magnifiers, lamps, writing guides, games, cassette recorders, and measuring devices.

Kaplan School Supply Corporation
P.O. Box 609
Lewisville, NC 27023
(800) 334-2014

Learning materials for early childhood.

Lakeshore
P.O. Box 6261
Carson, CA 90749
(800) 421-5354

Curriculum materials for infants and for preschool, elementary school, and special education students.

Library Reproduction Service
1977 South Los Angeles Street
Los Angeles, CA 90011
(800) 255-5002

Large-print textbooks, laboratory manuals, study guides, tests, and reference and general reading materials. Enlargements on request. Different type sizes available.

Lighthouse Industries
36-02 Northern Boulevard
Long Island City, NY 11101
(800) 453-4923

Vision assessment supplies; magnification aids.

LS&S Group
P.O. Box 673
Northbrook, IL 60065
(708) 498-9777 or (800) 468-4789

A variety of products for independent living, including magnification aids.

Maxi Aids
42 Executive Boulevard
P.O. Box 3209
Farmingdale, NY 11735
(516) 752-0521

A variety of devices for physically handicapped people, including talking calculators, magnification screens for televisions, and computer keypads with enlarged letters.

National Association for Visually Handicapped
3201 Balboa Street
San Francisco, CA 94121
(415) 221-3201

A variety of large-print books in such categories as literature, language, mathematics, reading, science, social studies, spelling, and leisure reading; pamphlets about visual impairments.

Recording for the Blind
20 Roszel Road
Princeton, NJ 08540
(609) 452-0606

Books and other educational materials on tape, free on loan to people who cannot read standard print because of visual, physical, or perceptual impairments. Books in major fields of study recorded on request.

Scholastic
2931 East McCarty Street
P.O. Box 7501
Jefferson City, MO 65102
(800) 325-6149 or (800) 392-2179 (in Missouri only)

Educational software for preschool and elementary school students.

Science Products
P.O. Box 888
Southeastern, PA 19399
(800) 888-7400 or (800) 222-2148 (in Pennsylvania only)

Adaptive aids for visually impaired people, including recorders, audio equipment, calculators, measuring devices, and magnifiers; large-print books.

Seeing Technologies
7074 Brooklyn Boulevard
Minneapolis, MN 55429
(612) 560-8080

A variety of video magnifiers.

Smith-Kettlewell Institute of Visual Sciences
2232 Webster Street
San Francisco, CA 94115
(415) 561-1619

Vocational and educational aids for visually impaired people.

SRA
P.O. Box 4000
Allen, TX 75002
(800) 843-8855

Instructional and educational assessment materials.

TeleSensory Corporation
P.O. Box 7455
Mountain View, CA 94039
(415) 960-0920 or (800) 227-8418

A wide variety of technological equipment, computers, and computer-related products, including video magnfiers, embossers, the Optacon, and software programs.

Organizations Serving Visually Impaired People

A wide variety of organizations disseminate information helpful to you, your students, and their families. In addition, many organizations on the national, state, and local levels provide assistance and referrals as well as information; operate toll-free hotlines; and publish materials that are valuable sources of information for professionals and for consumers. You may choose to join some of these or to be on their mailing lists. Organizations that do not appear in the listing that follows may be included in the *Directory of Services for Blind and Visually Impaired Persons in the United States and Canada, 24th Edition,* published by the American Foundation for the Blind, which also lists service and volunteer groups.

American Association of the Deaf-Blind
814 Thayer Avenue
Silver Spring, MD 20910
(301) 588-6545

The American Association of the Deaf-Blind (AADB) is a consumer organization of deaf-blind persons. It is involved in advocacy activities and holds a convention annually for deaf-blind persons and their families.

American Council of the Blind
1155 15th Street, N.W., Suite 720
Washington, DC 20005
(202) 467-5081 or (800) 424-8666

The American Council of the Blind (ACB) is a consumer organization that acts as a national clearinghouse for information and has an affiliate group for parents. It also provides referrals, legal assistance, advocacy support, scholarships, and consultative and advisory services to individuals, organizations, and agencies.

American Council on Rural Special Education
Department of Special Education
University of Utah
221 Milton Bennion Hall
Salt Lake City, UT 84112
(801) 585-5659

The American Council on Rural Special Education (ACRES) specializes in services for exceptional students and their families living in rural areas. It distributes information, publishes a newsletter and a journal, and advocates for the rights of disabled persons.

American Foundation for the Blind
15 West 16th Street
New York, NY 10011
(212) 620-2000 or (800) 232-5463

The American Foundation for the Blind (AFB) provides a wide variety of services for blind and visually impaired persons and their families, professionals, and organizations and agencies. In addition to promoting the development of services and conducting research to determine the most effective way of serving visually impaired people, AFB operates the M.C. Migel Memorial Library, a special reference library on blindness. It publishes books, monographs, pamphlets, and periodicals in print and in recorded and braille formats and provides information about the latest technology available for blind and visually impaired persons through its National Technology Center. It also develops and sells special devices and appliances for use by visually impaired persons, manufactures Talking Books, and operates a toll-free information hotline. AFB maintains the following regional centers across the country as well as a governmental relations office in Washington, DC:

Eastern Regional Center
1615 M Street, N.W., Suite 250
Washington, DC 20036
(202) 457-1487

Serves Connecticut, Delaware, District of Columbia, Maine, Maryland, Massachusetts, New Hampshire, New Jersey, New York, Pennsylvania, Rhode Island, Vermont, and Virginia.

Midwest Regional Center
401 North Michigan Avenue, Suite 308
Chicago, IL 60611
(312) 245-9961

Serves Illinois, Indiana, Iowa, Kentucky, Michigan, Minnesota, Missouri, North Dakota, Ohio, South Dakota, and Wisconsin.

Southeast Regional Center
100 Peachtree Street, Suite 620
Atlanta, GA 30303
(404) 525-2303

Serves Alabama, Florida, Georgia, Mississippi, North Carolina, Puerto Rico, South Carolina, Tennessee, the Virgin Islands, and West Virginia.

Southwest Regional Center
260 Treadway Plaza
Exchange Park
Dallas, TX 75235
(214) 352-7222

Serves Arkansas, Colorado, Kansas, Louisiana, Montana, Nebraska, New Mexico, Oklahoma, Texas, and Wyoming.

Western Regional Center
111 Pine Street, Suite 725
San Francisco, CA 94111
(415) 392-4845

Serves Alaska, Arizona, California, Guam, Hawaii, Idaho, Nevada, Oregon, Utah, and Washington State.

American Printing House for the Blind

1839 Frankfort Avenue
Louisville, KY 40206
(502) 895-2405

The American Printing House for the Blind (APH) administers an annual appropriation from Congress to provide textbooks and educational aids for legally blind students. In addition to publishing braille and taped editions of a variety of books and magazines, APH manufactures special educational aids for visually impaired students and modifies and develops computer access equipment and software. It maintains an educational research and development program and a reference service providing information about other sources of educational materials.

Association for Education and Rehabilitation of the Blind and Visually Impaired

206 North Washington Street, Suite 320
Alexandria, VA 22314
(703) 548-1884

The Association for Education and Rehabilitation of the Blind and Visually Impaired (AER) is a professional membership organization that promotes all phases of education and work for blind and visually impaired persons on the local, regional, national, and international levels. AER conducts conferences, provides continuing education programs, publishes newsletters and a journal, and operates a job exchange and reference information service. It also certifies rehabilitation teachers, orientation and mobility specialists, and classroom teachers and contains several divisions in such areas as early childhood, elementary education, and orientation and mobility. It has a division for itinerant teachers.

Association for Persons with Severe Handicaps

11201 Greenwood Avenue North
Seattle, WA 98133
(206) 361-8870

The Association for Persons with Severe Handicaps (TASH) advocates for educational services for disabled persons. TASH disseminates information, publishes a newsletter and a journal, and acts as an advocate for the rights of people with disabilities.

Association for Retarded Citizens (ARC)

500 East Border Street, Suite 300
Arlington, TX 76010
(817) 261-6003

The Association for Retarded Citizens (ARC) works on local, state, and national levels to promote services, public understanding, and legislation on behalf of mentally retarded persons and their families.

Council for Exceptional Children

Division for the Visually Handicapped
1920 Association Drive
Reston, VA 22091
(703) 620-3660

The Council for Exceptional Children (CEC) is a professional organization for teachers, school administrators, and others who are concerned with children who require special services. CEC publishes position papers as well as periodicals, books, and other materials on teaching exceptional children.

Helen Keller National Center for Deaf-Blind Youths and Adults

111 Middle Neck Road
Sands Point, NY 11050
(516) 944-8900

The Helen Keller National Center for Deaf-Blind Youths and Adults provides services and technical assistance to deaf-blind individuals and their families and maintains a network of regional and affiliate agencies.

Library of Congress National Library Service for the Blind and Physically Handicapped
1291 Taylor Street, N.W.
Washington, DC 20542
(202) 707-5100 or (800) 424-8567

The National Library Service (NLS) for the Blind and Physically Handicapped conducts a national program to distribute free reading materials in braille and on recorded disks and cassettes to blind and visually impaired persons who cannot use ordinary printed materials. In addition, the service operates a reference section providing information on reading materials for disabled persons.

National Association for Parents of the Visually Impaired
P.O. Box 317
Watertown, MA 02272-0317
(800) 562-6265

The National Association for Parents of the Visually Impaired (NAPVI) is a membership association that supports state and local parents' groups and conducts advocacy workshops for parents of blind and visually impaired children. NAPVI operates a national clearinghouse for information and referrals and holds national and chapter conferences.

National Association for Visually Handicapped
22 West 21st Street
New York, NY 10010
(212) 889-3141

The National Association for Visually Handicapped (NAVH) produces and distributes large-print reading materials, acts as an information clearinghouse and referral center, and sells low vision devices.

National Association of State Directors of Special Education
2021 K Street, N.W., Suite 315
Washington, DC 20006
(202) 296-1800

The National Association of State Directors of Special Education (NASDE) provides assistance to state education agencies and offers consultative services. NASDE also publishes newsletters and sponsors conferences.

National Braille Association
1290 University Avenue
Rochester, NY 14607
(716) 473-0900

The National Braille Association is concerned with the production and distribution of braille, large-print, and taped materials for blind and visually impaired people.

National Coalition for Deaf-Blindness
c/o Perkins School for the Blind
175 North Beacon Street
Watertown, MA 02172
(617) 972-7347

The National Coalition for Deaf-Blindness advocates on behalf of the interests of deaf-blind persons and provides information to consumers and professionals.

National Federation of the Blind

1800 Johnson Street
Baltimore, MD 21230
(410) 659-9314

The National Federation of the Blind (NFB) is a consumer organization that maintains affiliates in all states and the District of Columbia and works to improve the social and economic opportunities of blind and visually impaired persons. It evaluates programs and provides assistance in establishing new ones, funds scholarships for blind persons, and conducts a public education program.

National Organization for Albinism and Hypopigmentation

1500 Locust Street
Suite 1816
Philadelphia, PA 19102
(215) 545-2322

The National Organization for Albinism and Hypopigmentation (NOAH) is a consumer organization that provides information on albinism, publishes a newsletter, and sponsors conferences.

National Society to Prevent Blindness

500 East Remington Road
Schaumburg, Il 60173
(708) 843-2020

The National Society to Prevent Blindness (NSPB) conducts a program of public and professional education, research, and industrial and community services to prevent blindness. NSPB has a network of state affiliates, and its services include screening, vision testing, and disseminating information on low vision devices and clinics.

Office of Special Education and Rehabilitative Services

U.S. Department of Education
330 C Street, S.W., Room 3086
Washington, DC 20202
(202) 205-5507

The Office of Special Education and Rehabilitative Services (OSERS) has federal oversight responsibility for special education services.

Recording for the Blind

20 Roszel Road
Princeton, NJ 08540
(609) 452-0606

Recording for the Blind (RFB) lends tape-recorded textbooks and other educational materials at no charge to blind and visually, perceptually, and physically impaired students and professionals. Recording is done in a network of studios across the country.

RP Foundation Fighting Blindness
(National Retinitis Pigmentosa Foundation)

1401 Mt. Royal Avenue
Baltimore, MD 21217
(410) 225-9400

The RP Foundation Fighting Blindness conducts public education programs and supports research related to the cause, prevention, and treatment of retinitis pigmentosa. It maintains a network of affiliates across the country and conducts workshops as well as referral and donor programs.

Appendix C Classification System for Materials

The following is a comprehensive numerical system for organizing materials, which you may choose to simplify or use as is. If your program already has many materials, categorizing them will be a major task, but you may well appreciate the results. As part of an effective organizational strategy, the materials should be grouped in your office according to category so they can be located easily. Maintaining a typed or computerized inventory will also facilitate locating needed materials.

000 Professional Library
001 Teaching techniques and theory
002 Learning activities
003 References (medical, low vision, ophthalmology, *Journal of Visual Impairment & Blindness*)
004 Resources for visually impaired persons
005 Awareness of disabilities
006 Mainstreaming/P.L. 94-142
007 Assessment
008 IEP writing
009 Media catalogs
010 Catalogs of adaptive devices and equipment

100 Mathematics, Social Studies, and Science
110 Math readiness
120 Basic skills
  121 Addition
  122 Subtraction
  123 Multiplication
  124 Division
  125 Fractions
  126 Problem solving
  127 Multiple skills
  128 Geometry
  129 Algebra and trigonometry
130 Practical mathematics
  131 Time, calendar
  132 Measurement
  133 Money
140 Manipulatives
150 Economics
160 Geography
170 History
  171 American history and government

172 World history and government
180 Nature/science
190 Health and safety
  191 Home economics (cooking, food, nutrition, sewing)
  192 First aid
  193 Eye education

200 Reading
210 Readiness
  211 Categorizing, classification
  212 Color and shapes
  213 Letter recognition
  214 Opposites
  215 Rhyming
  216 Sequencing
  217 Visual discrimination
  218 Concept development
220 Auditory decoding
  221 Consonants
    221a Initial
    221b Final
  222 Vowels
    222a Short
    222b Long
  223 Blends and digraphs
  224 General phonics
230 Comprehension
  231 Following directions
240 Multiple skills
250 High interest–low vocabulary
260 Structural analysis
  261 Syllabification
  262 Alphabetizing
  263 Affixes
  264 Compound words
  265 Context clues
  266 Sight vocabulary
270 Dictionary skills
  271 Library skills
  272 Study skills
280 General reading
  281 Braille
    281a Reading readiness
    281b Instruction
    281c Readers and reading series
    281d Texts
    281e Juvenile and intermediate
    281f Novels, adult
    281g Reference
  282 Large print
    282a Reading readiness
    282b Reading series and workbooks
    282c Texts
    282d Juvenile and intermediate
    282e Novels, adult
    282f Reference
  283 Regular print
    283a Reading readiness
    283b Reading series and workbooks

283c Texts
283d Juvenile and intermediate
283e Novels, adult
283f Reference

300 Communication Skills
310 Language development
  311 Vocabulary development
320 Written language
  321 Creative writing
  322 Grammar
  323 Handwriting
    323a Manuscript
    323b Cursive
  324 Spelling
330 Nonoral language
340 Listening skills

400 English as a Second Language
410 Foreign language

500 Vocational Skills
510 Elementary
520 Secondary
530 Survival skills (daily living, behavior)
  530a Driver's education

600 Self-concept
610 Self-concept for visually impaired persons and for people with disabilities

700 Assessment
710 Functional vision/vision screening
720 Auditory perception
  721 Auditory discrimination
  722 Receptive language
730 Visual perception
  731 Concepts
740 Educational assessments
  741 District and state tests
  742 Mathematics
  743 Reading
  744 General aptitude tests
  745 General psychological tests
750 Visual motor
760 Gross motor
770 Preschool/readiness
780 Behavior/social scales
790 Communication/oral language
  790a Developmental checklists

800 Perceptual/Sensory-Motor Skills
810 Fine motor
820 Gross motor
830 Orientation in space
  831 Body awareness
  832 Spatial relations
  833 Directionality
  834 Laterality

ITINERANT TEACHING

840 Visual perception
  841 Visual memory
  842 Visual motor
  843 Visual figure ground
  844 Visual discrimination
  845 Tracking
  846 Vision stimulation/efficiency
850 Auditory perception
  851 Auditory memory
  852 Auditory motor
  853 Auditory figure ground
  854 Auditory discrimination

900 Tactile Discrimination

1000 Orientation and Mobility
1010 Reference materials
1020 Mapping materials
1030 Mobility aids

1100 Visual Aids
1110 Magnifiers
1120 Monoculars
1130 Miscellaneous

1200 Music

1300 Typing

1400 General Games

1500 Braille Games

1600 Preschool

1700 Arts and Crafts

Reference Library

Reference materials containing useful information on visual impairments and related issues, blind and visually impaired students and their needs, and the education of blind and visually impaired students can be of invaluable assistance to teachers who work with these students. The following list of books, journals, and newsletters is a sampling of helpful materials for itinerant teachers.

BOOKS AND PAMPHLETS

American Foundation for the Blind directory of services for blind and visually impaired persons in the United States and Canada, 24th edition. (1993). New York: American Foundation for the Blind.

Attmore, M. (1990). **Career perspectives: Interviews with blind and visually impaired professionals**. New York: American Foundation for the Blind.

Ballard, J., et al. (1987). **Public Law 94-142 Section 504 and Public Law 99-457: Understanding what they are and are not**. Reston, VA: Council for Exceptional Children.

Barraga, N. (1983). **Visual handicaps and learning**. Austin, TX: Pro-Ed.

Barraga, N., Dorwood, B., & Ford, P. (1976). **Aids for teaching basic concepts of sensory development.** Louisville, KY: American Printing House for the Blind.

Berdine, W.H., & Blackhurst, A.E. (1985). **An introduction to special education** (2nd ed.). Boston: Little, Brown.

Bishop, V.E. (1986). **Identifying the components of success in mainstreaming.** *Journal of Visual Impairment & Blindness, 80,* 939-946.

Brennan, M. (1982). **Show me how: A manual for parents of preschool visually impaired and blind children.** New York: American Foundation for the Blind.

California Leadership Action Team for the Visually Impaired. (1985). **Statement of educational needs of visually impaired students in California.** Sacramento: California State Department of Education (available also from the American Foundation for the Blind, New York).

Curren, E.P. (1988). **Just enough to know better: A braille primer**. Boston: National Braille Press.

Davis, W.E. (1986). **Resource guide to special education: Terms/laws/assessment procedures/organizations** (2nd ed.). Boston: Allyn & Bacon.

Developing and maintaining a successful RP support group: A directory of ideas, articles and resources. (1985). Baltimore: Retinitis Pigmentosa Foundation Fighting Blindness.

Dodson-Burke, B., & Hill, E.W. (1989). **An orientation and mobility primer for families and young children**. New York: American Foundation for the Blind.

Erin, J.N. (Ed.). (1989). **Dimensions: Visually impaired persons with multiple disabilities**. New York: American Foundation for the Blind.

Falvey, M.A. (1986). **Community based curriculum: Instructional strategies for students with severe handicaps.** Baltimore: Paul H. Brookes.

Faye, E.E., & Hood, C.M. (1975). **Low vision.** Springfield, IL: Charles C Thomas.

Ferrell, K. (1984). **Parenting preschoolers: Suggestions for raising young blind and visually impaired children.** New York: American Foundation for the Blind.

Ferrell, K. (1985). **Reach out and teach: Materials for parents of visually handicapped and multihandicapped young children** (2 vols.). New York: American Foundation for the Blind.

Gallagher, P. (1978). **Educational games for visually handicapped children.** Denver: Love Publishing.

Goldman, C.D. (1987). **Disability rights guide: Practical solutions to problems affecting people with disabilities.** Lincoln, NE: Media Publishing.

Harley, R., et al. (1980). **Peabody model vision project.** Chicago: Stoelting.

Harrell, L. (1984). **Touch the baby: Blind and visually impaired children as patients—Helping them respond to care.** New York: American Foundation for the Blind.

Harrell, L., & Akeson, N. (1987). **Preschool vision stimulation: It's more than a flashlight! Developmental perspectives for visually and multihandicapped infants and pre-schoolers.** New York: American Foundation for the Blind.

Hazekamp, J., & Huebner, K.M. (1989). **Program planning and evaluation for blind and visually impaired students: National guidelines for educational excellence.** New York: American Foundation for the Blind.

Heward, W.L., & Orlansky, M.D. (1988). **Exceptional children: An introductory survey of special education** (3rd ed.). Columbus, OH: Charles E. Merrill.

Jose, R. (Ed.). (1983). **Understanding low vision.** New York: American Foundation for the Blind.

Kelman, C.D. (1983). **Cataracts: What you must know about them.** Boston: G.K. Hall.

Kirchner, C. (1988). **Data on blindness and visual impairment in the U.S.: A resource manual on characteristics, education, employment, and service delivery, 2nd edition.** New York: American Foundation for the Blind.

Kornzweig, A. (1981). **Diseases of the macula.** New York: National Association for the Visually Handicapped.

Leary, B., & von Schneden, M. (1982). **"Simon Says" is not the only game.** New York: American Foundation for the Blind.

Lewis, K., & Thomson, H. (1986). **Manual of school health.** Menlo Park, CA: Addison-Wesley.

Low vision questions and answers: Definitions, devices, services. (1987). New York: American Foundation for the Blind.

Lydon, W.T., & McGraw, M.L. (1973). **Concept development for visually handicapped children.** New York: American Foundation for the Blind.

Major, S., & Walsh, M. (1977). **Learning activities for the learning disabled.** Belmont, CA: Fearon Pitman Publishers.

Mangold, S.S. (Ed.). (1982). **A teacher's guide to the special educational needs of blind and visually handicapped children.** New York: American Foundation for the Blind.

Mellor, M. (1981). **Aids for the 80s.** New York: American Foundation for the Blind.

Mendelsohn, S.B. (1987). **Financing adaptive technology: A guide to sources and strategies for blind and visually impaired users.** New York: Smiling Interface.

Moore, S., Bensinger, S., Frere, S., & Dennison, A. (1984). **Bright sights: Learning to see.** Louisville, KY: American Printing House for the Blind.

Napier, G., Kappan, D., & Tuttle, D. (1981). **Handbook for teachers of the visually handicapped.** Louisville, KY: American Printing House for the Blind.

Olson, M.R. (1981). **Guidelines and games for teaching efficient braille reading.** New York: American Foundation for the Blind.

Pogrund, R.L., Fazzi, D.L., & Lampert, J.S. (Eds.). (1992). **Early focus: Working with young blind and visually impaired children and their families.** New York: American Foundation for the Blind.

Rex, E. (Ed.). (1989). **Print. . .braille. . .literacy** [Special issue]. *Journal of Visual Impairment & Blindness, 83*(6).

Rogow, S.M. (1988). **Helping the visually impaired child with developmental problems: Effective practice in home, school, and community.** New York: Teachers College Press.

Sacks, S.Z., Kekelis, L.S., & Gaylord-Ross, R.J. (Eds.). (1992). **The development of social skills by blind and visually impaired students.** New York: American Foundation for the Blind.

Scholl, G.T. (1986). **Foundations of education for blind and visually handicapped children and youth: Theory and practice.** New York: American Foundation for the Blind.

Scholl, G.T., & Schnur, R. (1976). **Measures of psychological, vocational, and educational functioning in the blind and visually handicapped.** New York: American Foundation for the Blind.

Schulz, C. (1983). **Security is an eye patch.** San Francisco: Sight Conservation Research Center and Northern California Society to Prevent Blindness.

Smith, A., & Cote, K. (1982). **Look at me: A resource manual for the development of residual vision in multiply impaired children.** Philadelphia: Pennsylvania College of Optometry.

Stein, H.A., Slatt, B.J., & Stein, R.M. (1987). **Ophthalmic terminology: Speller and vocabulary builder** (2nd ed.). St. Louis: C.V. Mosby.

Swallow, R.H., & Huebner, K.M. (Eds.). (1987). **How to thrive, not just survive: A guide to developing independent life skills for blind and visually impaired children and youths.** New York: American Foundation for the Blind.

Vaughan, D., & Asbury, T. (1980). **General ophthalmology.** Los Altos, CA: Lange Medical Publications.

Warren, D.H. (1984). **Blindness and early childhood development** (2nd ed.). New York: American Foundation for the Blind.

Willoughby, D., & Duffy, S. (1989). **Handbook for itinerant and resource teachers of blind and visually impaired students.** Baltimore: National Federation of the Blind.

JOURNALS AND NEWSLETTERS

AER Report
Job Exchange Monthly
Newsletter for Division XVI: Itinerant Personnel
Re-view
Association for Education and Rehabilitation of the Blind and Visually Impaired
206 North Washington Street, Suite 320
Alexandria, VA 22314

AFB News
Journal of Visual Impairment & Blindness
American Foundation for the Blind
15 West 16th Street
New York, NY 10011

Awareness Newsletter
National Association for Parents of the Visually Impaired
P.O. Box 317
Watertown, MA 02272-0317

The Braille Monitor
Future Reflections
National Federation of the Blind
1800 Johnson Street
Baltimore, MD 21230

The California Transcriber / CTEVH Journal
California Transcribers and Educators of the Visually Handicapped
741 North Vermont
Los Angeles, CA 90029

Exceptional Children
Council for Exceptional Children
1920 Association Drive
Reston, VA 22091

Exceptional Parent
P.O. Box 3000
Department EP
Denville, NJ 07834

In-Sight
Parents and Cataract Kids
P.O. Box 73
Southeastern, PA 19399

National Newspatch
Educators of Visually Impaired Preschoolers
Oregon School for the Blind
700 Church Street
Salem, OR 97310

Reflections Newsletter
American Council of the Blind Parents
c/o American Council of the Blind
1155 15th Street, N.W., Suite 720
Washington, DC 20005

Ruralink Newsletter
Rural Special Education Quarterly
American Council on Rural Special Education
Department of Special Education
University of Utah
221 Milton Bennion Hall
Salt Lake City, UT 84112

TASH Newsletter
The Journal of the Association for Persons with Severe Handicaps
Association for Persons with Severe Handicaps
11201 Greenwood Avenue North
Seattle, WA 98133

Appendix E

Sample Forms

Forms provide the means to standardize and organize information. Many of the forms used as examples throughout this book appear in this appendix as well, but they are blank instead of filled in. You may copy them as they appear or adapt them for your use. Readers are also encouraged to create other forms for which they see a need.

Book Order for September _____

Please return this form to _____ by _____

Please put this form in my mailbox or send it to me at _____
via school mail.

Thanks.

Student _____

Teacher of the Visually Impaired _____

School _____ Grade _____

Large Print _____   Braille _____

Title _____ Level _____

Author _____ Publisher _____

Copyright _____

	Office Use Only	
Source	Date Ordered	Date Received
_____	_____	_____

Title _____ Level _____

Author _____ Publisher _____

Copyright _____

	Office Use Only	
Source	Date Ordered	Date Received
_____	_____	_____

Title _____ Level _____

Author _____ Publisher _____

Copyright _____

	Office Use Only	
Source	Date Ordered	Date Received
_____	_____	_____

Schedule _____

Time	Monday	Tuesday	Wednesday	Thursday	Friday	Notes
8:00						
8:30						
9:00						
9:30						
10:00						
10:30						
11:00						
11:30						
12:00						
12:30						
1:00						
1:30						
2:00						
2:30						
3:00						
3:30						

Note: Dotted lines separate different activities at the same site.

To _____

Please complete this questionnaire and put it in my mailbox by _____.

Thank you.

1. Texts to be used in class:

Title	Author	Publisher	Copyright Date	Dates Used

2. I use $\begin{cases} \text{no} \\ \text{some dittos. (That is, work written in purple letters.)} \\ \text{many} \end{cases}$

___ 3. My worksheets sometimes involve print smaller than the size used here.

___ 4. I use the chalkboards, overhead projector, or films at least three times a week.

___ 5. I would like to learn how to enlarge worksheets using the office copier.

6. The best time to confer with me is

Day of week _____

Time/Period _____

Location _____

To: _____

Re: IEP for _____

Date: _____

Here is information that you may want to include in Part 1 of _____ 's
IEP:

I will be writing my own Part 2 and want to be present at the IEP conference. If possible,
please consider these preferences when scheduling the conference:

If you cannot schedule the conference at my preferred times, I will understand. Please let
me know as soon as the IEP date, time, and site have been confirmed.

Thank you.

To: _____

Re: _____

Date: _____

An IEP meeting for _____ is scheduled for _____ at _____

in _____. I realize it may be difficult for you to

attend but you may wish to give information to _____'s parent(s) about
his/her participation in your class.

Indicate below if you plan to attend the meeting and add pertinent comments. Please return

this form to my mailbox by _____.

Thank you.

Materials on Loan

Student _____ Year_____

School _____

Materials Loaned	Location	Date	Return Date	Transferred To	Date
1.					
2.					
3.					
4.					
5.					
6.					
7.					
8.					
9.					
10.					
11.					
12.					
13.					
14.					
15.					
16.					
17.					
18.					
19.					
20.					
21.					
22.					
23.					
24.					

Observation Summary

Student _____ Observer _____

Setting _____ Date _____

Time	Observations	Comments

Grade Summary

Student _____ Year _____

School _____

Period	Subject	Teacher	Room	Grade*						
				1st Q	2nd Q	1st Sem	3rd Q	4th Q	2nd Sem	Final

Notification of Itinerant Teacher's Absence

Please fill in the name of the teacher/office to be notified when you are absent.

Teacher _____   Year _____

Student	School	Person/Office to Notify

Academic Tests Summary

Student _____ Date of Birth _____

Test _____ Date _____

Scores:

Comments:

_____

Test _____ Date _____

Scores:

Comments:

_____

Test _____ Date _____

Scores:

Comments:

Student Checklist

Name _____

Teacher's Initials			
School Year	19 ___ to 19 ___	19 ___ to 19 ___	19 ___ to 19 ___

Teacher's Initials			
School Year	19 ___ to 19 ___	19 ___ to 19 ___	19 ___ to 19 ___

Program Referrals

Date	Name	Referred By	Investigating Teacher	School	Date of IEP or Closing		Reason for Closing

Student Data Card

Name _____   Parent(s) Name _____

Date of Birth _____   Address _____   Student I.D. # _____

Home
Phone _____   Emergency
Phone _____   Work
Phone Mother _____   Father _____

Year	Itinerant Teacher	School of Attendance	School in Resident District	Gr.	Special Class	Reading Level	BL PS	Print Used	Bus	Other

Gr. = Grade   BL = Legally Blind   PS = Partially Sighted

Student Data Card (side 2)

RFB # _____ LOC _____ Rehab. _____ Transit I.D. _____ SS # _____

Hospital _____ Doctor _____ Medical # _____

Eye Condition _____ Entered Program _____

Vision Reports _____ Low Vision Exam _____

_____

_____ O&M Received _____

_____

Acuity: _____ Other Handicaps _____

_____

_____ Comments _____

Psychological Evaluation _____

_____

_____

Passed Proficiency _____

Graduated _____

or Left Program _____

RFB = Recording for the Blind   LOC = Library of Congress   Rehab. = Department of Rehabilitation   SS = Social Security   O&M = Orientation & Mobility

Schedule for _____

Year _____

To all personnel: Please indicate the day and time you regularly use this room.

Time	Monday	Tuesday	Wednesday	Thursday	Friday
8:00					
9:00					
10:00					
11:00					
12:00					
1:00					
2:00					
3:00					

Date: _____

To My Substitute:

Please be aware that _____ is in my _____ period

class. _____ is a visually impaired student and reads

_____.

Please remember that

1. Anything you write on the board will need to be verbalized and,

2. During fire drills or disaster drills, you will need to take extra care to make sure this student is safe. I have made the following special arrangements to ensure his/her safety:

_____

_____

_____

3. Other: _____

_____

_____

_____

Should you have other questions or concerns, talk with _____

_____ here at the school, or contact

the teacher of the visually impaired, _____

at _____.

Sincerely,

Index

Absences, **73-74, 84-85**
Accommodations in schools, **69, 71-72**
Activities
  basic, **9-20**
  end-of-the-year, **37**
  in-service for teachers, **20-28**
Adapting materials, **12, 18, 40-41**
Aides
  See Assistants, Paraprofessionals
Aloneness, **82**
American Automobile Association, **84**
American Foundation for the Blind, **24**
Assessment of students, **18, 28-32**
Assistants, **6, 40, 86**
Attributes of itinerant teachers, **5-6**
Audiotape recorders, **54**

Boardwork, **40**
Books, **54**
Bosses, **86**
Braille, teaching students who use, **21-24**
  See also Adapting materials
Braillers, **54**

Calendars, **51**
California, **3**
Cars, **78-79**
  district, **72**
  maintenance of, **83-84**
  materials and equipment in, **78**
  See also Travel; Driving
Caseloads, **6, 9-11**
Certification of itinerant teachers, **7**
Classmates, programs for visually impaired
  students, **27**
Closings, unscheduled school, **84**
Color, in textbooks, **12**
Color-coding system, **14-15**
Community groups, programs for, **28**
Computerized equipment, **42, 53**

Conference-preparation period, **7, 15, 18, 71**
Consultation, **18, 32**
  with school personnel, **42-46**
Contracts, teachers' union, **6, 69**
Copiers, enlarging, **41, 54**

Dittos, **21, 40**
Driving, **83-84**
  See also Travel

Eclectic approach to establishing caseloads, **10-11**
Education for All Handicapped Children Act
  (P.L. 94-142), **4, 28, 81**
Effectiveness of teachers, **5-8**
Electric typewriters, **54**
Electronic magnifying devices, **54**
End-of-the-year activities, **37**
Enlarging copiers, **41, 54**
Enlarging materials, **12**
Equipment, **29**
  computerized, **53**
  specialized, **41-42**
"Exchange days," **82**
Extended year, **75**
Eye examinations, **36**
Eye report form, **36**

Faculty, relationship with, **67**
Family, working with a student's, **28**
Flexibility, **35, 39, 79**
Forms, **47, 56**
  See also Sample forms and letters

Geographic approach to establishing caseloads, **10**
Goals and objectives, of Individualized Education
  Programs, **28-31**

Handouts, **16, 40**
History of itinerant teaching, **3-4**
Home visits, **35**

Individualized Education Program (IEP), **4, 7, 16, 28-34, 39**
Individualized instruction, **39-40**
Information, how to organize, **47**
In-service programs, **20-28**
Insurance coverage (travel), **37**
Integration of visually impaired students, **39-46**
Isolation, **82**
Itinerant placement, **3-4, 6**
Itinerant programs, rural, **81-86**

Keys for school rooms, **69**

Labeling textbooks, **14**
Lamps, **27, 54**
Large print, **12**
Liability (travel), **37**
Lions Club, **28**
Locating offices and teachers, **77**
Lockers, students', **75**
Low vision devices, **54**
Lunch break, **7, 15, 20, 71**

Magnifying devices, electronic, **54**
Mailbox, teacher's, **69-71**
Mainstreaming, **6, 68**
Materials
    adapting, **18, 40-41**
    for itinerant program, **53-55**
    for teachers, **47-51**
Meetings, staff, **20, 53**
Monitoring, **7, 15, 31-32**

New Jersey, **3**
New teachers, **5**
Novels, **54**

Observations, **18**
    of students, **46**
Office space for itinerant teachers, **55**
Options, placement, **3-4, 6**
    in rural areas, **85-86**
Organization
    of itinerant program, **53-57**
    of materials, **53-55**
    of office, **55**
    of student data, **47, 56**
Orientation and mobility (O&M) specialists, **6, 22**

Paraprofessionals, **86**
Parking, **79**
Participation in the classroom, **35**
Pen pals, **82**
Philosophy of itinerant teaching, **3-4**
Phone chains, **85**
Placement
    in itinerant program, **3-4, 6**
    options, **3-4**

Preliminary preparations for establishing a schedule, **15-17**
Preliminary Scholastic Aptitude Test (PSAT), **29, 35**
Preparation-conference period, **15, 18**
Preparation time, **71**
Print size, **12**
Print, teaching students who read, **24-27**
    See also Adapting materials
Program options in rural areas, **85-86**
Program organization, **53-57**

Qualities of itinerant teachers, **5-6**

Raingear, **77**
Reading-writing stands, **54**
Recorders, audiotape, **54**
Reference books, **54**
Referrals, **56**
    assessment of, **18**
Reimbursement
    for faculty participation in in-service programs, **20**
    hotel, **85**
    mileage, **72, 78-79**
Relationship to faculty and staff, **67-68**
Residential schools, **3, 85-86**
Resource-room programs, **3**
Rights in schools, **69-72**
Role of itinerant teacher, **3, 7**
Rules and procedures, **68**
Rural itinerant programs, **81-86**

Sample forms and letters, **13, 14, 19, 22, 23, 24, 25, 26, 33, 34, 43, 44, 45, 48-50, 56, 58-65, 68, 70, 74, 75, 76, Appendix E**
Schedule, setting up, **15-20**
Scholastic Aptitude Test (SAT), **29, 35**
School personnel, consultation with, **18, 42-46**
Seating, classroom, **21**
Simulation of visual impairment, **27**
Software, **42, 78**
Specific-level approach to establishing caseloads, **10**
Staff
    for itinerant program, **9-11, 55**
    meetings, **20, 53**
    relationship with school, **67-68**
Standardized testing, **35**
Stands, **27, 54**
State schools, **3, 85-86**
Stopwatches, **54**
Storage of materials and equipment, **71**
Structure, for itinerant teachers, **5**
Students
    integration of, **39-46**
    observation of, **46**
    participation in in-service programs, **20-21**
    scheduling, **17-18**
Study trips, **36-37**

Substitute teachers, **74**
Summer school, **75**
Supplies, **47**
Support systems, **6**

Taped materials, **12, 40**
Teacher assistants, **86**
Teacher organization, **47**
Testing, standardized, **35**
Textbooks, ordering and providing, **11-15**
Transcribers, **6, 7, 32, 40**
Transition from high school, assistance for, **31**
Transparencies, **40**
Transportation, **36**
   See also Travel
Travel, **36-37, 71, 83**
Travel time, **18, 71, 83**

Typewriters, **54**
Typing stands, **54**

Union contracts, teachers', **6, 69**
Unscheduled school closings, **84**

Vehicle, **78-79, 83-84**
   See also Cars, Travel
Visual impairment, simulation of, **27**
Voice synthesizer, **42**

What Do You Do When You See a Blind Person (film),
   24
''Windshield'' time, **83**
Work space
   for itinerant teachers, **15**
   for students, **12, 21**